growing simple

by
Jim and Mary Competti
copyright © 2016

EDITOR
Carton Rider

FOREWORD BY
Carlton Rider

DEDICATION:

We dedicate this book to our parents, who taught us the value of hard work, the importance of family, and to never be afraid to fail.

In honor of those same values instilled in us by our parents, we in turn dedicate this book to our four children: Loryn, Aaron, Wes and Nolan. We hope to inspire you to follow your own passions in life and work hard to fulfill your dreams. But most importantly, have fun doing it!

Cover photo credit:
Africa Studio/Shutterstock

Table of Contents

Foreword

Foreword by Carlton Rider

I remember the picture as if it was taken yesterday. It was this bluish-white sphere, suspended in the blackness of space over the moon's horizon taken on December 24, 1968 by the Apollo 8 crew. For the first time, humans saw a picture of planet Earth taken from space and it was spectacular!

This was long before the effects of global warming, pesticides, preservatives, and issues dealing with air and water pollution would become topics of conversation and scientific study. Back then, we didn't give much thought to our responsibility for maintaining the delicate balance between Mother Earth and its inhabitants while respecting the rights and privileges of all creation.

It would be decades later before those in the medical and scientific communities would begin to suspect that perhaps there were certain causes, some of which were thought to be man-made, for the increasing rates of certain cancers, cardiovascular disease, and diabetes among those living in developed nations where there was an overuse of antibiotics in animal feed, the use of fossil fuels for fertilizers and agricultural chemicals, and the need for extensive food transportation because of centralized food production.

Although many of these studies are on-going and may take years to reach well-researched conclusions, there is a growing body of evidence to indicate that what we eat and how this food is produced and preserved, does have an effect on our health and, more importantly, that each of us has control over what we eat, how that food is grown and preserved and how we can learn to overcome the daily stresses of life by living a simpler and more healthy life-style.

Mark Hyman MD, in his book *Eat Fat, Get Thin*, says "Making our own food allows us to take back our power. We have become food consumers, not food producers or makers, and in so doing we have lost our connection to our world and ourselves."

In their book, *Growing Simple*, Jim and Mary have shared how striving for a simple lifestyle has given them an opportunity to experience life to its fullest. The fact that so many of you from around our country and other countries throughout the world read, appreciate, and respond to their weekly blog is testimony to the fact that you, too, are eager to return to a simpler lifestyle and to be able to eat more healthfully.

There is much more to this book than just gardening. In a sense, this is a love story, not just between Jim and Mary and their journey toward a more simple life, but also their love of our fragile planet Earth and the importance of maintaining that delicate balance between providing for our needs while respecting all that Mother Earth has to offer us.

Reading *Growing Simple* is captivating, informative, and thought-provoking. Humor is laced throughout the book. There's the incident about tearing down the roof of a barn that would eventually be rebuilt as the center-piece of the farm. There's the episode about the bats and the time the mother bee wouldn't be accepted by the other bees in the hive. There's the story about the initial clearing of the land that would be in the beginning of the Farm project which reminds one of the pioneer days.

There are chapters that explain how to make compost, creating and maintaining raised rows beds, how to plant tomatoes (using the famous stake-a-cage), peppers, onions, lettuce, and other vegetables to ensure a bountiful harvest. You will also find information on canning so that you can enjoy the fruits of your labor throughout the year in addition to a variety of recipes.

If you want to plant and enjoy fresh vegetables but live in a large city within a confined area, don't worry! You will read how you can have luscious vegetable garden by using pots of various sizes and other types of containers on your patio or deck. Nothing is impossible if you really want to enjoy farm freshness!

You will find two chapters especially interesting! They aren't necessarily about gardening per se. Chapters 12 and 13 are about life and finding the time to do what is really important to each of us and how we can overcome the failures that will most surely come along life's journey of making dreams into realities. Although both Jim and Mary have their own full-time professional careers, unrelated to the Farm, in addition to keeping up with their four children's busy schedules, they share how they are able to maintain a balance in their lives between their first love... the Farm, and the demands of their professional careers.

Many times dreams begin with the simple phrases such as: What if...? What would it be life if...? Could we....? After throwing around some ideas, things begin to happen. Suddenly, what seemed impossible becomes a reality.... clearing an over-grown field; building a barn and chicken coop; some landscaping; a small vineyard...

a garden. Lucky for us that Jim and Mary decided to share their dream of a simpler life with the world so that we, too, might have the opportunity to make simplicity a part of our own lives.

- chapter one -

Bats in the Belfry

The infamous Cardington barn

There we were, just the two of us together on a hot, sweltering summer day in the middle of July, attempting to tear down a hundred-year-old barn - piece by piece. The year was 2011. It was just the previous fall that we had started the journey to create our little farm and homestead.

We hadn't expected to build our farm's barn until at least the fourth or fifth full summer, but opportunity had knocked in the form of a Craigslist ad. The offer was simple and straightforward – a couple was in need of someone to tear down their old barn to make room for a new driveway and whoever answered the call was more than welcome to haul away all of the precious wooden beams, boards and metal roofing for free!

That someone, of course, became Mary and me. It really didn't matter that we had no clue how to tear it down or where to begin, we just knew that all of that beautiful old barn wood would be exactly what we needed to build our own farm's barn – and it was free!

We had spent the better part of the first few days removing the barn siding and flooring and by now the barn had been reduced to a beautiful timber frame-like structure. Now it was time to tackle the job we both had put off as long as we could – removing the old metal roof.

The plan hatched was simple enough – I would climb up the insanely slippery 30 or so feet to the peak of the old roof, straddle the roof line and remove the top roofing nails. Mary, meanwhile, would remove the bottom set of nails by standing on the highest step of a rickety old wooden stepladder placed safely, of course, on a bed of a borrowed 24' flatbed truck so she could reach the bottom of the panels. Hopefully, if all went well, the 28" x 16' long panels would slide down easily one at a time.

That was the plan anyway. After what seemed like an eternity to simply work the nails of the first panel loose, I yelled down to Mary to give a pull, fully expecting to see that first sheet of roofing metal slide easily down to the earth below. But after a gentle pull, followed by a stronger tug, the panel wasn't budging. It seems that people really did build things better and stronger in the old days!

So with that we decided that if we perhaps gave a set of really strong pulls together, it would come free and that's when the real fun began.

"Okay," I stated, "on the count of three....one, two, three," and we both began to pull. After about 2 seconds of hard pulling I quickly realized I was in big trouble!

"Stooppp!!!!" I bellowed out to Mary below above the crashing noise of corrugated metal bending and twisting. "Stoooppppp!!!!!!" I screamed again - this time much louder and with a much more convincing fervor. The entire barn was moving, and it wasn't from a rare Ohio earthquake.

As the swaying slowly ceased – I looked down at Mary, clearly showing a little fear in my eyes and lowering my voice from my prior screams, and gently muttered "Did you not feel the entire barn moving?"

"Not really," she said laughing. I think she was somewhat proud that she might just have the strength to bring the whole barn down. I, on the other hand, was a little more concerned perched up on top. So I slowly tugged on the metal and the barn once again swayed..."wow...that's not good," she said in a very calm matter.

Unfortunately, it seemed that our removing the walls and floorboards did nothing to loosen the metal roof panels but did wonders in making the entire barn structure unstable.

Sensing the entire structure would come down with me on top of it if we continued the hard pulling effort we went to plan B. I would cut the panels free of the boards below with a reciprocating saw. It seemed plausible enough and, after Mary had handed up the saw to me, the sharp construction blade on the saw made quick work of the old nails and panel number one slid to the earth.

For a brief moment – and I do mean very brief – we had that momentary, self-congratulating, pat-on-the-back thought of success. We had overcome the problem and were on our way!

And then it all changed. As I moved on to cut the second panel loose all of those happy feelings and smiles turned quickly to blood-curling guttural screams as a slew of bats flew out from underneath the second panel and within centimeters of my head. It seems that our beloved empty barn was still home to a large population of bats!

I'm not really sure to this day how I ended up down on the ground level beside Mary in less than 5 seconds – but I did, screaming all the way. In fact, I'm pretty sure that I set a world record for speed ladder descending that day.

So there we stood, looking up at the roof and laughing uncontrollably at the melee that had just unfolded, knowing full well that we probably had a few bats in our own belfry for even attempting to dismantle the old barn ourselves – let alone build a new one from it!

But we were working together at following our dream of creating a simple and self-sufficient farm and lifestyle from scratch - and most importantly - having fun doing it!

It was a dream born from our shared love of gardening, cooking, and DIY – and one that ultimately would create Old World Garden Farms.

chapter two

How We Became Jim and Mary

Before we go any deeper into our story, it's important to take a moment to know a little more about us and how we came together to be Jim and Mary.

When we sat down to write this book, we knew very well this would be the hardest chapter to complete, but also the most poignant and meaningful to the entire story.

We can both write and talk all day long about gardening, our farm, our goals, chickens, bees, recipes or any other thing that covers the topic of Old World Garden Farms. It is easy. It is what we know. It is what we care about. It is what we love.

But it's quite different when we sat down to write a section together about our relationship and how it all came to be. We realized instantly that it is hard to put into words what we share and how lucky we are. I don't want to ever say we take for granted what we have together, but we both realize how fortunate we are to have crossed each other's paths.

People that hear us speak or meet us for the first time usually ask if we were high school sweethearts. They point to the fact that we share so much in common, that we do everything together, and that we are so at ease with each other.

Yes, every single one of those statements is true. But the whole truth is that until we met, we both went through some difficult times in our own lives. I think the key for both of us, and something we always try to pass on to others, is that no matter where you are in your life, and no matter what situation you face, you can face it with a positive attitude and an open mind. I really think, in a nutshell, that is what helps us tackle anything.

Mary and I grew up less than 30 miles apart – but it wasn't until later in life that we were fortunate enough to have our lives finally come together. We were actually both married in 1993, just not to each other.

Yes, like many Americans, we are a blended family, and every day we realize how incredibly fortunate we are to have each other and four kids that have blended and bonded so well together.

We laugh at how many times our paths probably crossed without ever knowing it. We both played sports at rival catholic high schools at the same time and we know that there had to be many times we were watching and rooting against each other. It gets better – both of our first marriages were performed by the same priest, which happened to by my Uncle, who also baptized both of our first born in the same church without either of us knowing it.

Sometimes we wonder how we never officially met, but all good things come to those who wait. For us, it was only fitting that for two people who grew up loving sports, it was their children's sporting events that finally brought them together. We met at a basketball game, and the rest, as they say, is history.

When Mary and I finally met it was instant. We realized from the moment we first spoke to each other that we were simply meant to be. I can't describe it, and neither can Mary.

We are one. We believe in each other. We believe in ourselves. We know that at the end of the day, no matter what has happened, that we will be there for each other. Together, that bond has carried us through thick and thin. There are not many sentences that we can't finish for each other, and not many ideas we don't at least agree about in some shape or form. I think what makes us strong as a team is that we are both very strong individuals.

We have so very many people to thank for our positive outlook and attitude and for helping to make our own dreams become a reality. The list is full of siblings, relatives and close friends who helped shape our lives – but without fail – it all started with our parents.

Each of our parents helped shape our formative years with an emphasis on working hard for what you want and what you believe in. They didn't just talk the walk – they walked it.

We are both so very blessed to have had 4 parents who were never afraid to get their hands dirty, and who made sure we got dirty as well!

Both sets of parents gardened, canned, and loved to share family meals. They planted those seeds in us at an early age. They exposed us to the wonders of our own backyards. Whether it was time spent in the garden planting and harvesting, or even the dreaded chores of weeding, we learned valuable life skills while breathing in the fresh air of the great outdoors.

The list could go on and on – mowing, raking leaves, planting trees or helping in the flowerbeds, but the simple fact is our parents taught us both the beauty of nature and the value of a little hard work and sweat. They taught us how to grow our own food – and more importantly – that it was okay to get our hands dirty.

Yes – like most kids with those memories, I think we can both be honest and admit that at the time we might not have appreciated our mandatory participation in the assigned chores, but I can tell you they laid the groundwork for what we love today.

In addition to all of that, they taught us it was okay to make mistakes. And that it was far more important to keep our heads up and learn from those miscues than to hang them in defeat. We have both made mistakes, had success, failure, and everything in between. And we will continue to do all of those with gusto. It is who and what we are about and why it is so important to the story of Old World Garden Farms.

It is an example that we both hope that we are passing down to our own children as well. And with that – you know a little about us.

Okay....deep breath. We are both very glad this chapter is complete. Let's get on with the story of Old World Garden Farms!

chapter three

And So It Begins...The Clearing of the Land

The overgrown field mowed off and ready to go

The humble beginnings of a little farm, a new life, and a new lifestyle.

I don't think I will ever quite forget the start of our little farm. It was Friday, October 8th and the year was 2010. The cool, crisp, clean air of a gorgeous early Fall evening in Ohio is hard to beat – and this one was perfect! With the early evening sun beating down, we pulled up to our future "farm" with nothing more than a trailer and a rented walk behind brush cutter ready to clear the land to begin our life together.

Before we get to that fateful October weekend when the farm first truly began – we actually need to back up a few months to where the idea of having that little farm all started.

Mary and I had been together quite a while, and by mid-summer of 2010, one thing we knew for certain is that we were simply made to be together. Over the few years we had come to know each other, she had often spoke of a little piece of property that she had owned a few miles on the outskirts of town. It was late that summer when she finally first took me to see it.

We had wanted to do something together, something that could be "ours", and the blank canvas of a parcel of land was the perfect match to create a space together.

"I think I had it mowed off a year or two ago – but it's just a big open field...nothing really much to it at all," Mary told me as we made our way down the road to the property. As we pulled up the little half-overgrown driveway to the top of the hill overlooking the land below, I realized that the term "a year or so ago" might have been more accurately described to be 3 or 4 years. Small trees and brush had overtaken the landscape –

and the grass leapt over the car as we pulled in and stopped.

But much like our life has been ever since, we could certainly see the forest, or in this case the future farm, through the trees. Looking down over that overgrown patch of a jungle – for better or for worse - we decided to make it our project together.

I think by the time we had driven back to town, we had already decided that we wanted a big garden the next year, and to someday have chickens, a barn and what the heck – while we were in the mood to dream - a house together! And on that fateful ride home – that is when and where we decided to start to build our life and our dreams.

Clearing the Land...

I remember the day like it was yesterday. October 8th 2010. It was our first day ever of working on our little farm together! We had rented a self-propelled Billy Goat walk-behind brush cutter with a miniscule 24" cut, rolled it off a rickety old trailer that I had from long ago and started clearing the land! The first cut was quite comical as we walked down together behind the machine, trying carefully to keep our footsteps within the tiny cutting swath as to not get swallowed up by the brush.

After what seemed like an eternity, we finally made it to the bottom of the field and turned around to look back up. You couldn't even tell where we had mowed! The tall brush and grass on either side of the little 24" cut path had been swallowed up by the brush on either side. I think we realized then and there that this would be an all-weekend project!

We worked until dark that night, clearing a small spot at the top of the hill so that we could at least sit out a couple of lawn chairs and a cooler to have the rest of the weekend.

On Saturday, we arrived back early in the morning to start up again and, for the rest of the weekend, we took turns walking laps around the land with the Billy Goat. Those early treks around the property took about 10 to 15 minutes; enough time for one of us to rest on the chair while the other took their turn. The only break from the monotonous drone of the engine was the occasional scream coming from somewhere down the hillside when Mary would see one of the hundreds of mice and other vermin scurrying from the oncoming mower. And so it went. Lap after lap and tank after tank of gas - our weekend was spent in hard labor! And we couldn't have been happier.

Finally, by Sunday evening, with our muscles sore, our faces burnt from the sun, and our legs and arms covered with cuts and abrasions from the countless thorns piercing our bodies, we mowed off the last strip!

It would be the first of many days and nights we would leave the farm totally exhausted - but fulfilled. It was the start of our dream together! It was also when we completely realized that together, we could accomplish anything.

chapter four

The Chickens Arrive at The Farm

From the moment our field was cleared, we began to think about everything we wanted to grow and raise on our little farm. First and foremost, we knew we wanted chickens!

Like almost all individuals who consider raising their own chickens, we couldn't wait to head out to a little coop and collect our own "farm-fresh" eggs! Just the thought of being able to wake up someday and create the perfect breakfast of fresh eggs, home-grown potatoes and a slice or two of toasted homemade bread was enough to make us both jump for joy!

Yes, we knew in addition to those great tasting fresh eggs that there would be additional benefits, but we could never have imagined just how incredible of a role the chickens would play in making our self-sustaining farm a success. In fact, the chickens have become and will always remain the Rock Stars of our farm!

The process of raising a few backyard chickens is actually quite simple. In as little as 5 minutes a day we easily water, feed and collect the eggs from our small flock of hens. It really comes down to the ability to provide the basic necessities of life – food, water, and shelter – and a little space to keep them happy.

You don't need a rooster, and in fact, if you are raising them for eggs, it is far easier without a rooster. As far as noise is concerned, without the cackling rooster, hens are fairly quiet except for the few happy chirps they make to proudly proclaim that they have just laid an egg.

They quite simply are the ultimate multi-purpose farm animal. Beyond those great tasting eggs (and they are amazing), our chickens provide us with our best and most powerful compost ingredient –

chicken manure! Chicken manure is high in nitrogen, and when we clean out the coop, that high nitrogen content along with the shredded straw is the perfect base to creating a hot compost pile.

In addition to the compost, we make and use a high potent, all-natural fertilizer from their manure. If you steep a 5-gallon bucket for a day or two along with a shovel full of fresh manure the resulting liquid is a powerful instant miracle-growing fertilizer for plants. We use that mixture to boost our young plants when they first begin to grow in our garden, and the results are amazing. As a word of caution, manure tea can be extremely rich and can burn leaves and plants when put directly on them. For this reason, we use it as a watering agent to soak the soil around the base of the plants.

The benefits don't stop there. Along with the eggs, compost and fertilizer, a flock of chickens will do wonders in keeping insect populations in check! Chickens, by nature, are scratchers - loving to root around the soil to find all kinds of bugs and worms.

Each and every fall, after the summer garden has been cleared, we turn the chickens loose to peck at the soil. They scratch around and help clear the garden of many of the insects that can take their toll on our plants, including the larvae of such bugs as Japanese Beetles and moths that are left in the soil to return the following season.

While they are scratching around they also feast on any weed seeds they might discover, helping us control that issue as well.

The insect control extends well beyond the garden. When we first moved to the farm, ticks were rampant. In fact, you could hardly work for a few hours without finding at least one climbing up to attach somewhere on your body. Fast forward five years later and it is a rarity to find a single tick around.

Like I said – our hens really are the Rock Stars of the farm!

The First Coop – Strange Looks From The Neighbors

When we first decided to raise chickens at the farm we had a couple of large initial obstacles to overcome. First, we had to find a source for the chickens. Second, we had to build them a home.

It was in the early spring of 2011 when we figured it was time to get busy building our first coop. With no power at the farm, we decided to construct it in the middle of the driveway at our mainstream suburbia home.

The weather was beginning to warm a bit, and after the long cold winter, several couples in the neighborhood had decided to take up walking as a form of exercise. As the couples would walk by each evening, we would get comments such as "looking good", or "keep up the good work!" Most, we realized, had no clue what we were building.

It wasn't until the actual outside structure was nearly complete that we started getting more curious looks and more direct questions like. "Ok, you have to settle the bet, are you building a playhouse or a dog house?"

To their surprise, and maybe a touch of initial horror, we would laugh and tell them that it was actually a chicken coop. That, of course, was always followed by a quick clarification from us of "Don't worry, it's not staying in the driveway, we are moving it out to our farm."

It is important to say that at this point of our journey our kids were a bit embarrassed that we were building the coop in the driveway. They had not quite embraced this whole "farm" concept yet.

We live in a small enough community where the head football coach of our high school lives just up the street. Without hesitation, one day at school he approached one of our boys and commented, "Son, you are going to have the most elaborate dog house on the block." To the horror of our son, he shyly admitted to

Coach that it wasn't a doghouse at all, but a chicken coop in progress.

Mary and I firmly believe that part of parenting is making sure that you can keep your kids humble and embarrass them from time to time – mission accomplished!

Building The Coop On A Budget

That first coop was a test run for what the farm was to be all about. We wanted to prove we could build our dream of a self-sufficient farm and garden without spending huge amounts of cash. More importantly, to do it using free or low-cost recycled and reclaimed materials, all while keeping it aesthetically pleasing to the eyes. That first coop was proof that with a little elbow grease and hard work, we could do it!

The entire frame was created from salvaged 2 x 4's and pallet boards, with ½" thick reclaimed pine shipping crate boards used for the finished siding. The egg boxes and roofing deck were made from salvaged plywood torn out of the shipping crates and we finished it all off with some left over shingles we already had on hand.

Yes, it took a bit of time to get all of the nails out of the pallet and shipping crate boards, but in the end, we had a pretty cool looking coop without spending hardly any cash to speak of.

A few weeks later, much to the happiness of the kids – we loaded the coop up on a rickety old trailer and placed it out at the farm.

Our First Chickens

We started this chicken venture with only the knowledge we could glean from books and on-line research. We had both had a little experience in our past being around chickens, but certainly not as the owners!

We purchased our first set of chicks (6 Leghorns and 3 Golden Comets) from a local farm store. As we brought them home, I think we both realized that we had just committed full force to this "farm thing" and there would be no looking back.

For the first 8 weeks of their life, chicks need to be kept in a brooder. A brooder is nothing more than a temporary home that keeps them safe and warm until they feather out and are ready to take on the world. Keeping with our low cost recycling theme, we made our brooder from a few scraps of 2 x 4's and chicken wire. We set it up in the basement and attached a heat lamp to keep the temperature around 90 to 95 degrees during the baby chick's first 5 to 7 days. And then we set about doing what every newbie chicken farmer does – worry!

We worried and watched for all of the bad things the books and the internet told us might happen. We checked the temperature every hour or so and fretted if it went a little too high or low. We would pick up the chicks and make sure the dreaded chicken butt paste syndrome wasn't affecting them. We would dunk their little beaks into the water to make sure they were all learning to drink properly and we must have changed their water every hour that first week to make sure they would stay healthy. Guess what – they did! And we have come to find out in the subsequent years that although all of those things might happen at some point – in reality – baby chicks tend to really not need too much help from us to figure it all out. It turns out that this whole chick to chicken thing has been happening for thousands of years and if you just provide the basic necessities of food, water and shelter they do okay.

It's actually amazing to watch how quickly baby chicks learn to use the water and feeder troughs. As our little girls grew over the next few weeks, we became very proud parents. We would take them out in the front yard and let them walk around and watch the double takes of neighbors driving by. I am sure, during that period of time, we had many convinced we were the "crazy tree hugging people" of the neighborhood.

Baby chicks go through quite a metamorphosis during their initial growth. They start out as adorable day old fuzzy chicks. They then turn to a very ugly and awkward stage during weeks 3 to 6 – almost looking like aliens from another planet. It's not until about the 8-week mark that they start to actually look like what we all know as chickens.

As our first set of hens feathered out at that critical 8-week mark it was time to move them to the farm.

It would be the understatement of the year to say we were absolutely terrified the first time we locked them in for the night in their new digs at the farm. We both imagined marauding animals like coyotes, raccoons, foxes and hawks would be conspiring during the overnight hours to break into the coop and steal our girls.

But once again, our fears had little basis. The chicks settled in at the farm just fine and the coop provided perfect protection from the aforementioned creatures. We proudly named every single one of hens of that first flock, giving each of them a name to describe their unique characteristics and mannerisms. And yes – chickens do develop hilarious personalities and traits – it is simply wonderful to experience and see firsthand.

Big Mamma's name was derived from her large and gentle stature. Curious George received her name because of her penchant for needing to be wherever we were to see what we were doing. Sherwin Williams gained her name by spending most of her life pecking paint off of everything and anything she could find it on, and Amelia Earhart was the flyer of the group, making it a game to hop up on ladders and then see how far she could glide.

The First Egg

As they grew and developed, our thoughts turned to the day we might get our first egg from our hens. Depending on the breed, most hens will initially lay somewhere between weeks 18 and 22.

As our chickens were heading into the 17th week of their existence, Mary's parents came to town for a visit from Florida. It was Saturday morning, and we decided to take them out to see the girls and the farm. As we walked into the coop – there it was! A single tiny egg the size of a ping pong ball sitting proudly in one of the nesting boxes! Now, it wasn't much to look at (the first eggs never are), but it made no difference to us – we were now officially chicken farmers!

Devastation...And A New Coop

Everything went beautifully the first two years. The chickens were happy. They were laying large amounts of tasty eggs, and the entire process of turning fresh manure into incredible garden-building compost was in full swing. It then abruptly changed in the early spring of 2013.

I was out of town on business when Mary called. I could tell instantly by the sadness in her voice that the news was not good. Mary had opened the door of the coop, only to find Big Mamma had been senselessly killed, decapitated with no other signs of trauma.

Two nights later – it happened again. George was next, followed by Sherwin Williams. One by one, something was killing our chickens and we had no idea what! The coop was completely secure and the run was surrounded by 1" x 2" welded wire, which even the tiniest of raccoon couldn't fit through.

We tried everything. First we set out live traps each night, but the only thing we caught was our neighbor's cat. He would drop his head each morning as we let him out, almost to say, "Yep, I guess I should figure out when I go in there that door is going to close behind me."

Finally, after talking to a local Ohio Department of Wildlife Officer, we came to the conclusion that the culprit was most likely a mink. Minks can get into very small openings – and one look at our 1" x 2" wire in the chicken run was more than enough to convince the wildlife officer that a mink was the issue.

That single mink destroyed our entire first flock, always figuring a way to dig under or around every single thing we tried to put in place to stop him.

We were bound and determined to figure a way to keep him out in the future and Coop #2 quickly became our project for the spring of 2013. We had already been contemplating a bigger coop over the prior winter. We wanted to expand the flock to about 12 to 18 birds – and needed a bigger space to accommodate them.

It was the mink disaster, however, that sped the project up. I told Mary it was my personal goal to never let her find a chicken killed in our coop again and I set out to build Fort Chicken Knox.

We again used a lot recycled materials to keep the cost down. We were able to build the entire frame from scrap 2 x 4's and the bottom walls were reclaimed metal roofing sheets we cut down to match the barn. This time, though, the security was upgraded!

We covered the entire floor with ½" x ½" wire mesh to keep out the tiniest of creatures. On top of that we added 8 inches of packed limestone dust that hardens to near brick-like consistency. We put that same mesh in the windows, doubling it up for an extra layer of protection. Finally – we built an entire cement block foundation from reclaimed cinder blocks to create an impermeable fortress for our girls.

Thankfully, as of the writing of this book, our chickens have remained safe! As for the old coop – we actually donated it to a gentleman who wanted to start his own little flock. After some remodeling to make it a bit more secure it is still going strong today!

I can honestly say that it is nearly unimaginable for us to ever think there will come a day when we don't have our own chickens. They have been incredible for us in so many ways, and our farm simply wouldn't be the same without them!

chapter five

The First Garden at the Farm

A day's harvest from our first garden in 2011

Anyone who has ever gardened knows the excitement and anticipation of the few months leading up to planting day each year. Flipping through the endless colorful pages of the seed catalogs that fill your mailbox while the snow is gently falling out the window - one can only dream of what harvest season may bring.

For us, the experience was heightened as we neared the Spring of 2011, knowing it would be the first garden we would ever plant at "the farm" – a place we someday hoped to call home.

Looking back now, I don't quite think we realized how many obstacles we faced trying to plant that first year. For starters, when it came to equipment, our arsenal consisted of a shovel, rake, post-hole digger and the four hands attached to our two bodies. Adding to the difficulty was the fact that we had no running water – an issue we would have to come to grips with soon enough. Finally - with no fence or barrier between our plants and the wide-open field around us, we were faced with the possibility of growing produce for the native critters and not our plates.

We had both settled on the fact that it would probably take nothing short of a miracle to have any kind of success that inaugural year. Our first big decision to face was where to locate the garden. The 3 acre property consisted of a long narrow strip of land with sloping hills and a valley in between. The top of the hill at the entrance was off limits – knowing it would have to be reserved for our future house. The middle valley portion posed a problem as well. It seemed that any heavy rain turned it into a flowing river at the drop of a hat. So with that, we were left with the slight sloping ground at the back of the property as our only option.

Creating Our First Raised Row Bed

I would like to be able to say that we knew that raised rows were the answer from the beginning, but in reality, they were born purely out of necessity! With no way to break up the hard grass and soil for the garden – and with time running short that first Spring - we decided to build our growing rows on top of the earth.

Using only straw and a single truck load of pulverized topsoil, we constructed twelve 18" wide by 20' rows on top of the grass. We first laid down 6-12 inches of loose straw to form the 18" wide rows. We spaced the rows about 30" apart to create a path for working the growing rows. Then, ever so slowly and wheelbarrow by wheelbarrow, we poured pulverized topsoil over each row of straw to create our first raised row beds.

When it came to planting day, my dad's old trusty post-hole digger became the star of the show. Its funny how sometimes pure necessity leads to invention – and in the case of the post-hole digger – it couldn't be more accurate.

I travelled up and down each raised row and plunged the post hole digger in every 24" to create a 6" to 8" deep planting hole. The post hole digger created a perfect space for planting in just seconds – and to this day has become the way we plant our vegetable plants every year.

As each hole was created, we would fill in the bottom few inches with compost – and them drop in the plant and fill back in with an equal mixture of the existing soil and more compost. Once planted – we then mulched around each plant with a little more compost. This double use of compost – both in the planting hole and on top as a mulch has really helped with our garden's success over the years. The compost in the hole helps to feed the vegetable plants as they begin to grow – and also keeps the soil loose and friable – allowing it to soak up and hold moisture. When used as a mulch on top, it not only helps to deter weed seeds from forming near the plants, but as with all mulches, it also helps to insulate and regulate the soil temperatures from the hot days and cooler nights. More importantly, every single time it rains or we water – those nutrients in the compost are then leached down into the soil and taken in by the roots of the vegetable plants. It is a win-win!

The problem that first year was that we had no home-made or home grown supplies of compost readily available. We initially made do by purchasing a few organic bags, but compost can be expensive so we had to be careful to use it where it was needed most.

All of those first year garden challenges – the lack of tools, a ready-made garden space, and zero homemade compost – combined to teach us how important it was to concentrate our limited resources and efforts on the small space where the plants actually grow. It is a practice we continue today, which not only helps us to conserve on resources, but the time it takes to manage our entire garden. It also taught us the value of having our own compost pile – one of the reasons we now have a minimum of two going at all times.

As amazing as it seems, with our little raised rows and that trusty old post hole digger, we were able to plant the entire garden that first year in under 30 minutes. When we finished, we covered up all of the walking rows with straw to help keep down the weeds, sighed, and called it a day.

Expecting The Worst

With no fence and no protection for our little garden, we somewhat expected the worst. We went home that first night after planting day and neither of us slept well at all. I think we both had nightmares that somehow, every living creature was coming out to gnaw down our precious plants. We had visions of showing up the next day with every plant sacrificed as a big bountiful feast for all of the deer, groundhogs, raccoons and other wildlife that were sure to have been spreading the news that a garden had been planted solely for them.

We arrived early the next morning with our hearts pounding. It was a beautiful day and actually quite warm for the month of May. As we turned in and up the small slope that looked down over the farm, I could hardly stand to look down at the garden, imagining our beautiful vegetable plants were most likely yanked from their holes in an all-out wildlife dinner fest. But as we approached the garden, there were all of our plants unharmed and untouched by anything or anyone. They had made it through their first night unscathed! However, the early May heat was stressing them out.

And as one fear was put on the backburner, the next fear took its place. How in the heck are we going to water 90+ plants each day?

That first garden consisted of 45 tomato plants, 45 pepper plants, 3 cucumbers and a few zucchini plants along with a single row of purple green beans. It became quite apparent that they were all going to need water and we had not a drop of it on the farm. With no well, we were going to have to figure out how to water – and fast.

But hey – we are doers and problem solvers – so we did the only thing we could do. We went home and collected as many jugs as we could find, filled them with water, transported them back to the garden and proceeded to water by hand. Surprisingly it didn't take very long to accomplish this once seemingly overwhelming task. We once again learned the value of conservation with both of us directly watering only at the base of every plant to maximize our efforts.

Our watering routine went on all summer long, carrying crates of milk jugs filled with water each and every time Mother Nature wouldn't cooperate with her own supply.

There were some speed bumps, of course. Like the day we left the filled water jugs back at the house. Instead of making the 20-minute trek back we took a five-minute drive down to a nearby creek, took off our shoes and socks and filled some containers we had left at the farm from the bone chilling stream. It may not have been perfect, but where there is a will there is a way!

We look back now on those early watering days and laugh at it all. Yes, it was a lot of effort and a bit crazy – but we made it work! It also led us that winter to come up with a permanent solution - a simple rain water collection system that we placed on the gutters of our new barn that has since supplied any and all watering needs at the farm.

So, with the watering issue solved, we were on to the next challenge with our first garden at the farm.

The Birth of the Stake-A-Cage

With about 45 tomato plants and 45 pepper plants in the ground and growing quicker than imagined, we realized we needed to give them some support - and FAST! After suffering sticker shock at the prices of commercial tomato cages and stakes in the store, we knew we needed to come up with a DIY plan that wouldn't break the bank.

With some left over welded wire fencing from the chicken coop run and a few 2x4s left over from building the coop, we went to work trying to make our own supports. We sawed the 2 x 4s in half with our table saw and then cut them down into 3' and 5' stakes. Next, we cut the fencing panels into 18 inch x 24 inch sections and attached them to the homemade wooden stakes with a few u-nails. And bingo – our Stake-A-Cage Tomato supports were born!

After we put a few up we started realizing that we were on to something! Not only did they go together easily, they looked great and had a lot of advantages over the commercial cages and old wooden stakes that we had used in the past.

For starters, it combined the best of the two old ways used to tie up tomatoes; using the strength of strong wooden stakes with the ease of a wire trellis cage. By keeping the wire grid flat and not making a true cage, it was easy to tie up each branch as needed and made harvest time a breeze. The 5' stakes worked perfect for our large tomatoes – and the 3' sections held up the peppers with ease.

With the watering issue resolved and the plants supported with our newly created Stake-A-Cages the garden season was in full swing and even we were surprised with the results! In fact, from that little 20' x 40' plot of land, we harvested well over 2,500 pounds of tomatoes, peppers, cucumbers and zucchini in that first year alone. By the end of August, friends and family tended to shy away from us, knowing we would be begging them to help take the ever increasing loads of daily produce off of our hands. We canned, froze and cooked more fresh produce that year than we ever imagined and we were hooked on raised row gardening.

That year taught us that the raised row method was the way to go and it became the basis of our gardening system. We realized that we could grow so much more than just those initial crops - and quite possibly the majority of the food that our family consumed. And the ideas began to flow on how we could expand next year's garden to help feed our family.

chapter six

Why Do It All?

Countless numbers of people continuously inquire about why we do what we do. We frequently get asked, "Why do you spend your time gardening, canning, and building things that you could buy?" or "Why did you start documenting your journey through a blog?" But there is no doubt that the question that we receive the most and several times a day is "How do you find the time?"

The best way to answer these questions is to learn a little more about our history, how we grew up, and where we are now in our lives.

We both grew up in families that spent a countless number of hours in the garden and in the kitchen. Throughout our childhood we hesitantly worked alongside our parents pulling weeds, snapping beans, and hauling produce to the sink. We didn't necessarily enjoy those chores, but we realize today that it helped form who we are and it is one of the main reason why we do what we do.

As children we had memories of sitting down with our families every night and enjoying a homemade meal as we talked about the events that happened that day. We ate slowly, enjoyed each other's company and solved what seemed were all of life's problems at the dinner table. We both were assigned chores before dinner in helping with the gathering of food or setting the table and of course, doing the clean up afterwards.

We both came from families that worked hard to provide what we needed. That often meant working a couple of extra jobs, fixing things instead of buying new things, and being thrifty sometimes just to make ends meet. This required each family member to contribute to the success of the family by doing chores, taking care of each other and being grateful for what we had. This also taught both of us that working hard for what you want in life was normal, not the exception.

Fast forward several years and life has significantly changed for both of us. We both work full time, and between the two of us have four very active children. Every night we were pulled away from home to transport someone to practice, attend a sporting event, or volunteer for a school function. We often ended up eating dinner on the road, in the car, or at 8 o'clock in the evening. We knew that this wasn't how we wanted our kids to remember their childhood.

I remember the day that our life would take that unexpected change like it was yesterday. It was 10pm on a Thursday evening. We both were exhausted from the work week, not being home until after dark every day and eating out every meal that week. From the ball park hot dogs to the pizza we would pick up on the way to the next event, we simply felt miserable. We finally looked at each other that night and agreed that we needed to make a change, and immediately! We needed to step back and take control of what we could and develop a sense of balance in our lives. To us, that meant the building of our farm and our future.

From that moment on, every free moment we found, we would head to the farm to complete even the simplest of tasks – haul some rock, transplant ornamental grasses or just feed and water the chickens. If we didn't have the time to drive there, we would be discussing, planning, and developing ideas to make our dream a reality. As we sat at the ball fields patiently waiting for the game to begin or sitting for countless numbers of hours during a never-ending rain delay, we would make our list of what food we wanted to can from the produce out of our first garden or discuss what the next step should be in pursuing the creation of the farm.

By the end of 2011 we were exhausted! We had successfully harvested several hundred pounds of produce from our very first garden, built a chicken coop and pergola and tore down two barns to begin building our own. We were sore, beat up and began to rethink if this was really the 'simple life' that we envisioned. We knew we had to keep focused and when one of us was questioning if we would ever achieve the dream of living the simple life we had to be there to reassure each other that we were still on track in working towards that goal. And that is when the development of the blog came to fruition.

My brother, who lives several states away, had started a personal blog that he shared with just our immediate family members in order to keep in touch. On occasion he would write an article to reflect personal thoughts, feelings, hopes and/or disappointments about a certain event that had occurred. Some say it was by mere coincidence that on one of those days that he had shared an article that he had written with us, both Jim and I were questioning the purpose and direction on the development of our simple life at the farm. I believe that in life things happen for a reason – and I thank my brother every day for unknowingly sending us on to the next level of our journey.

After reading his most recent reflection on life through his own words we decided that it would be beneficial to document the progress of our farm. This would allow us an opportunity to reminisce on how far we had come, to recall the progress that we have made, and would provide us an avenue for an up-to-date, photo documentary on the transformation from what the farm looked like on that first October day when we were faced with an empty field of tall brush to the beauty that it has become today. But most importantly it would allow us to keep focused on with our goals to live the simple life that we had in mind. A secondary purpose was to develop a way that would allow our family members who are spread across the country to keep them up to date on what projects we were working on and a way for them to 'visit' the farm through pictures. In return, they would then be able to help us stay on track by holding us accountable for the progress and completion of the projects that we began.

So there it began. We made the leap to initiate a blog over the winter of 2011 to help us stay motivated and to share the journey with our family. In the beginning, and to this day, it really has helped us to stay focused on working toward our dreams. It is amazing, when you put down in words your goals, aspirations, and desires, you have a much stronger sense of accountability to achieve them. Couple this with photographs of where we started and where we are today, it keeps us motivated to continue towards our dream, even on those rough days. However, we had no idea that our tiny little blog would become so much more than that.

A couple of weeks after we began posting articles and pictures, Jim discovered that someone from North Carolina began 'following us'. At that time, we only had family members that had subscribed to receive our posts and we had no idea why someone that we didn't even know would be interested in what we were doing in rural central Ohio.

And then it began to expand – every day we would have new followers from across the United States and eventually other countries. We quickly realized that we were not alone in our journey to get back to wanting a life that was filled with real food, a sense of simplicity, and the building of a dream using your own two hands. We learned so much from our followers through comments, emails and suggestions.

Quickly we realized that we were making a difference in lives around the world. We received messages from several people who we helped inspire to fulfill their goals: the young couple who wanted to start gardening and had no idea until they read one of our posts how to get started; the elderly couple who used to love to garden but gave it up a long time ago because they could no longer till the ground and who now decided that our raised row gardening was perfect for them; and the individuals who gave up on their own dream because life became too complicated and now are returning to the journey to live a more simple life.

For us, it is and will always be, a work in progress. But each day it gets a little better, feeds us a little more, and makes our future a little more certain. We are more committed than ever to live with a simpler approach to life. As the farm continues to progress into the reality that was once a thought, idea and dream, our focus remains the same, to build a simple life that focuses on being responsible for ourselves, our environment, and to give back to others.

So, when friends ask us why we work so hard at building our future, we usually just smile and say: "It's never work; it's what we love to do." And that truly is who we are and why we do what we do.

chapter seven

Dreaming of a Barn

Our recycled barn

Crazy! Looking back now and realizing the effort and, in some cases, pure luck that it took to create our barn. There is no doubt at all that we were crazy for thinking we could pull it off. Somehow we did.

Our barn will always be the centerpiece of our little farm. It stands for just about everything we believe in: frugality, recycling, DIY, learning from the past and building for our future. When people speak of something truly being a labor of love, all I need to do is think of our barn project and I understand exactly what they mean.

The idea for our barn's look came from a simple pencil drawing sketched out over the winter of 2010-2011. We had cleared the field the previous fall and were all set to start with our first batch of chickens and a garden in the spring.

If I could bottle the energy and anxiety that we both had over the winter months that first year, I am pretty sure we could power an entire city. We were so anxious to begin "The Farm" and it seemed like those dark, cold and grey winter days would never move on so that we could get started. That energy and anxiety led us to a lot of daydreaming and planning on those long winter days. One of those daydreams became that "someday" barn we wanted to build.

We knew exactly what we wanted –and what we didn't. As useful and economical as modern pole-barns can be, we knew that it wouldn't be the right fit for our little farm. We wanted a barn that looked like a barn; one with the character and distinction of a structure that had stood on that very spot for years; one with wood that looked worn and aged - but beautiful. An interior that was open and airy, with vaulted rafters and a loft instead of low hanging 2 x 4 trusses.

With visions of future barn parties and farm-to-table dinners shared with family and friends, we craved an outdoor entertaining space as well. Perhaps an attached pergola or an outdoor kitchen, but whatever it would be, had to fit our vision of an all-natural farm. In a nutshell, we wanted to create a rustic, beautiful, old-world barn for our farm.

Of course, we also knew that all of this "wanting" was WAY out of our price range and budget – but when has that ever stopped someone from dreaming? So dreaming it was. While we waited for winter's clutch to break its ugly hold, we let our minds wonder to the possibilities, including the addition of an attached pergola and outdoor kitchen. We would talk about different thoughts and ideas each night, until finally, after a month or so of going back and forth, I took a pencil and sketched out a simple drawing. Although my artistic skills leave a lot to be desired, that one simple pencil drawing brought our barn to life. When it was finished we slapped the drawing up on the refrigerator and spent the rest of the winter dreaming about our "someday" barn.

From a financial standpoint, we knew there was no way we would be able to build it for at least a few years. We were adamant about sticking to the original goals for the farm – the first of those being taking on zero debt. In holding true to our goals, we knew that we wanted to create our barn space with reclaimed lumber and salvaged materials. Especially since that would allow us to have that worn and rustic look that we so desired. Although the story goes much deeper, in essence, our barn is the marriage of two old barns, each having had a useful and productive previous life. One of the barns was the infamous bat barn that we found through a Craigslist posting. The other was a much more sentimental structure: a barn built by my father that had been a fixture on my parent's property for the past 40 years.

I will be the first to tell anyone we are not barn builders. We did a lot of things completely backwards. As an example: who puts up finished walls before the rafters are installed? Even better, who starts hanging signs in the barn for decoration without a roof? Well, we did, and somehow we were still able to complete our barn.

We built things when we could and as we found or could afford the materials needed. That being said, it didn't always follow traditional building plans. But we had a vision and we stayed the course with a lot of help and advice from friends and family.

We recycled and re-used everything we could. The old barn roof became our new barn's lower siding, while we used old barn flooring to make our new doors. Through it all, and I don't think either of us can still tell you exactly how, we were able to build our barn a few years earlier than we ever expected.

The Story of Two Barns...

The Cardington Barn

For all that is said about the dangers and pitfalls of Craigslist, I have to say that our new OWG barn would never have been built without it. Not only did we find the Cardington barn via an ad, but we were also able to sell all of the old beams and boards that we couldn't use in our barn project to pay for most of what we didn't have on hand for ours. The Cardington Barn was simply an answer to our prayers.

Looking back now, it was definitely a bigger undertaking than we had initially thought. We spent countless hours and weekends travelling back and forth to deconstruct it piece by piece. But beyond the bats, beyond the blood, sweat and tears that it took to tear it down, we learned about how much we truly were capable of doing. Yes, many times during the process we had no clue what we were doing but we persevered. We learned. We kept at it and we made it happen. It taught us that no matter the size or scope of a project – if you Bar– you can accomplish anything. It is a lesson that continues to help us each and every day.

Dad's Barn

A month or so after finishing the Cardington barn tear down, Mary and I began to take down my father's old barn. My dad's rustic red barn had a past and a story of its own to tell. You see, my Dad had actually deconstructed that very same barn from a relative's property almost 40 years prior in the fall of 1973.

My father, with the help of my uncle and a couple of my sister's high school and college boyfriends, took apart each board and rebuilt it piece by piece. And that barn stood strong all through my childhood and it stayed there until Mary and I took it down 40 years later to give it a new life once again.

My father passed away when I was just 12 so it was an incredible process for me to see Dad's handwriting on some of the beams and walls where he had painstakingly marked each board to put it back together. I love what building this barn has taught Mary and me. We have worked side by side every step of the way during the building process and that is a memory no one can ever take from us.   I'm sure there are many barns of the past that were built by family members that have that same type of connection and it makes me proud to know we are carrying some of that past into our future.

I love our new "old" barn. Every single time I drive into the farm and see it, I smile. I remember working through those hot days with Mary tearing down the old ones to make it. I remember all of the scrapes and cuts and bruises building it. I remember Mary about to kill me as I asked to lay out the squaring lines "just one more time to make sure we got it right". And through all of the hard work I remember the great friends and family who helped us tear down and re-build it into "our" barn. I remember all of the laughter and all of the fun that went into it.

It was a lot of hard work and yes, all of that work saved us a lot of money. But more than anything, I get to remember my father every time I look at it – and that is priceless.

- chapter eight–

What's all the Buzz?

Our first hive at the farm

As our visitors stroll into the entrance of the farm, one of the most popular areas of interest is our bee hives. It seems like everyone is fascinated with our hives which often leads into a detailed discussion about the intricate lives of bees, and their daily routines, not to mention, the honey that they produce. To say the least, we are far from bee experts, but like most things that we do around the farm; we continue to learn as we go.

When Jim mentioned that we should expand our farm by adding honeybees, my heart began to palpate. Now this was not in pure excitement and joy in anticipation that we would finally be able to help pollinate the crops at our farm, nor was it the idea that somehow we would be helping the world from the dwindling bee population. It was simply because I am allergic to bees. Was this finally his ploy to get rid of me and take over the farm himself? Did he really want to put bees right by the entrance of the garden where I spend most of my time during the summer? I knew that eventually we would want to try our hand at keeping bees at the farm. Not only would it help our vegetables, flowers, fruit trees and grapes to pollinate, but we would also be the lucky recipients of our own fresh honey from the hives.

We were fortunate enough to have a local bee keeper completing a weekly seminar on the tricks and tips of establishing your own apiary in a neighboring city. Unfortunately, with our crazy schedule and kids sporting events, we were not able to attend the full series. In fact, we only had one Saturday morning available out of the 6-week span where we were able to attend. Desperate to learn as much as we could, we contacted the bee keeper and begged him to let us attend the one day that we had available. Lucky for us, that presentation included how to set up your very first bee hive. Although we would have been better off attending the entire program, we knew that this opportunity would help us get started in this crazy, yet exciting, adventure.

After a lengthy phone conversation discussing our experiences, or lack thereof, and our plan to purchase bees in the spring, he agreed that we could, and definitely should, attend his class. That cold and bitter Saturday morning, Jim and I were so excited to take the first steps into the journey of becoming bee keepers that we ended up being the first ones there. In fact, we were so early that we had to wait in our car until someone arrived to open the door to the building. That didn't bother us though. We considered it an additional opportunity to talk to the presenter without taking the time away from anyone else.

We spent our first "bee" class, with a longtime area beekeeper named Mike. Although we had both spent the last 6 months reading up in every way possible about how to prepare and care for bees we knew that nothing substitutes hands on knowledge passed down from an experienced beekeeper. You could tell after just a few minutes talking to Mike how much passion he has for the art of keeping bees and that he truly enjoys passing that knowledge and passion on to others who are interested.

We talk about it a lot, but the generosity and helpfulness of people never seems to amaze us. As we spoke to him at the end of class, he even offered to help us release our first bees into the hive that spring. Over the course of the next week we ordered our hive box and beginners tool kit. Not to mention a bee keeping suit including an extra vail and gloves so that we both could be involved. And, oh yes, don't forget about an extra EpiPen to keep close by in the barn!

In May of 2013 we received the package of bees and within a few hours we officially gave ourselves the title of "beekeepers".

All in all, the once thought of daunting procedure of removing thousands of bees that had just traveled hundreds of miles into their new home at the farm went fairly smooth. It took only about fifteen minutes to open the package, remove the queen and bees and place them into the hive. We had both gone over the process of hiving the packaged bees a hundred times in our head – but that doesn't mean we weren't a little nervous heading to the farm with about 8,000 bees in a box in the trunk!

Knowing that being calm is a good thing when working with bees, we did our best to stay relaxed (or at least pretended to be relaxed). We put on the bee suits and went to work. We had installed the base and bee-hive structure the previous day in a semi-protected area along a tree line at the farm. All we had to do now was open the box, remove the queen cage, dump the remaining bees into the hive, and then hang the queen at the top of the hive.

Typically, the queen comes with the bees in her own little "cage" suspended from the top of the bee package. On one end of the cage is a wooden plug that, once removed, reveals a hard sugary substance. The entire cage is hung in the new hive, and the worker bees will slowly eat the sugar and release the queen. The time that it takes for this process to occur allows the bees and the queen to become familiar with each other. This introduction is crucial in preparing the hive to accept and welcome the new queen into their home.

About the only hiccup in the whole process was when Jim was opening the shipping box of the bees, he dropped the queen box into the swarm of bees below. Needless to say, the bees were not very happy at that point! But as they began to fly around us we tried hard to remember the words of our beekeeping mentor that "calm is good". We kept reminding ourselves that we both were fully protected. Jim slowly reached in, removed the individual cage, and then continued on by dumping the remaining bees into the hive. Next, he suspended the queen and her cage between the frames, closed it up, and celebrated that we made it out of there alive!

We then were able to set up a feeder filled with a syrup solution made from one-part water and one-part sugar. It provided the new colony with some nutrition while the bees became familiar with their surroundings and began to collect and bring back pollen to the hive.

Just about 24 hours after we had released the bees into the hive we could already see them flying in and out exploring their new surroundings. The bees will find pollen sources within a few miles surrounding their hive location. They then return to their new home and complete a sort of 'dance' that signals to the other bees where the pollen is located. It is amazing how the bees communicate with each other and are so precise when developing the honeycombs in the traditional hexagonal formation.

The following day we opened the hive to make sure the queen had been released. We suited up, pulled off the hive cover and inspected the small cage. To our chagrin, and honestly somewhat of a disappointment, she was still in her cage. Being new to bee-keeping, we were anxiously awaiting the release of the queen, like it would be broadcasted all across the county – The queen has been released!   We sadly hung her back up and closed the top of the hive. We returned two days later, a full 72 hours after she had been introduced to her new colony. We suited up one more time fully expecting her to be with the others, enjoying her new home. She was not, she remained comfortably in her cage. Now we were worried! We made a call to bee instructor Mike and you could actually hear him grinning through the tone of his voice. Now you two quit worrying! You just have a lazy queen!

Lazy isn't a word that we are used to hearing around our farm. How in the world did we end up with a lazy queen?? Mike told us to check back in a few days and if she wasn't released then we would have to release her from the cage ourselves. Being slightly impatient, the next morning, not a few days later, we checked again and we were glad to see that she finally had decided to join the others.

Our honeybees and hive had a good first year at the farm and we noticed a significant difference on the amount of produce that was harvested – most likely due to the bees' ability to pollinate the crops. We didn't gather any honey for ourselves that first year, as the bees needed it for food over the cold winter months.

Once the cold began to arrive, we had to figure out what we needed to do to protect them. Honeybees do not hibernate, instead they opt to cluster together to form a protective ball around the all-important queen. As they cluster, they move and fan their wings to increase the temperature of the hive and keep the queen safe and warm.

For our part, we inserted a reducer into the main hive body to keep out cold drafts and help to deter small mice or varmints that might try to rob the honey stored inside. Since this was the first full year for our new hive in addition to leaving all of the honey in place for them to have for winter use we also provided them with a supplement of food at the top of their hive in case of a long and cold winter. The honey and supplement was what they would consume to have the energy for all of that wing flapping and temperature control.

The honeybees also have a system to help prepare their hive for winter. They spend a lot of time inspecting the hive and sealing up tiny cracks and holes with propolis – a sticky thick substance they secrete to seal out the winter. They have also reduced their overwinter population by forcing a large majority of the male bees out into the cold to die. It may sound harsh – but the male bees perform no work related duties in the hive, and are simply not needed through the winter months.

If the temperature rises above the 50 to 55 degree mark at any point throughout the winter some of the bees will forage out and about to make what are called cleansing flights. This helps to keep the inside of the hive clean. Beyond that, they stay in that tight cluster awaiting the arrival of spring, much like humans except we spend it clustered in blankets near a warm fire!

The benefit of keeping bees however goes far beyond just the amazing honey we get back from our hive. They also play an important part in our farm's future success by helping to pollinate all of our fruit trees, grapes, blackberries, strawberries, flowers, and of course, our vegetable garden! Let's face it, without bees our world would be a pretty barren place!

So, with that in mind we decided to increase our hive from just one to three the next year. In fact, if we had to give any advice to someone who is considering raising bees for the first time it would be to start with at least two right from the start. Why? For one thing, establishing a new hive can be tricky – and if you start with only one and it does not survive you are back to square one! Even the best and most experienced bee keepers lose hives, some to pests, some to disease, and others still to a poor queen or a host of other potential reasons. Keeping multiple hives not only protects you from losing your bees entirely, but gives you great reference points to compare activity from one hive to another making you a more informed and thus better beekeeper. Besides, if everything goes well, you have a bit more honey to distribute to all those friends and family members asking for a jar.

Our bees are very lucky that there are very few commercial farmers close to the farm. This is crucial because although the bees have plenty of pollen at the farm, they will travel to surrounding areas to gather pollen from other crops as well. If commercial farms use pesticides and/or insecticides, the bees may gather this poison as they return the pollen to the hive, which in turn may cause illness and/or death.

This really wasn't much of an issue for us until April 2015. Jim was completing spring time chores at the front entrance of the farm when an unfamiliar vehicle pulled into the driveway. A gruff man exited the truck and immediately turned to Jim and pointed to the bees. "Are those your bees down there (by the garden)?" he asked. Jim responded affirmatively. "You are going to have to move them," he said with a firm, bold voice.

Immediately Jim became defensive. Who is this man telling us that we had to move OUR bees which were located at the back entrance of OUR garden? The man informed us that he had rented the land behind our farm from our neighbor just a few yards from our bee hives and planted soybeans the day before. The next day he was planning to spray commercial Round Up to kill all the vegetation in order for the GMO soybeans to sprout through the untilled field of grass.

We were devastated! All we could think about was that this would most likely kill our bees and possibly destroy our chemical free garden. We experienced a variety of emotions that week – first anger. We had worked so hard over the past 4 years to establish our dream. We have provided a safe home for our bees, used no chemicals in our garden and now that all could be ruined – and for what? Could a rented piece of property that had a few acres of soybeans planted on it really be the end to our dream?

Then arrived the sadness. Now we are going to have to relocate the bees away from the garden where they were so successful and comfortable. Now we might lose them all and our garden might now have chemicals running into it.

That's when reality hit. Just like everything we do at the farm, we got right to work. We leveled off a space about halfway up the hill to relocate the hives across the driveway near our small vineyard. We called various agencies – department of agriculture, lawyers, and organic farming agencies to see what could be done. We received countless numbers of emails from our blog followers around the world supporting us – through words, offers of compensation to try to buy the land, and from prayers for a peaceful resolution.

Unfortunately, the damage was done quicker than we could get an answer or resolution. We arrived at the farm the next day only to see, what we now call the angry farmer, spraying vegetation killer within yards of the back of the property which once held the bees, but also was the home to our asparagus, garden, and chicken coop. We quickly locked the chickens into the coop to avoid over spray and began video recording the events that were occurring. As the angry farmer drove past, with the spray pouring out of the back of the tank placed several feet above the ground, he looked at us and waved.

It was at that moment, that I knew we were fighting a battle that had no immediate resolution. There was nothing more we could do except provide soil samples, crop harvesting reports and document every time the spraying occurred along with the weather conditions on the day on which it happened.

The bees were moved and the hives blended into the landscape like they had been there for years. We planted the garden that year with hopes that chemicals didn't creep their way into the vegetables, and we kept the chickens confined to an outdoor run, in fear that they would peck at the vegetation of the property line which now was dying from the spray.

Luckily, we found out in the fall of that year that the land was purchased by another neighbor and we were assured that there would never be another GMO seed or poisonous spray there ever again. We are happy to announce that the bee hives will continue to remain at the farm and will be full of life again for years to come.

chapter nine

Food for Our Future

If you already garden, chances are when you read the list below you might chuckle a little as you think about the pleasures gardening can bring. Whether growing your own food in containers, on a windowsill, as potted plants on a patio, or in a big garden plot in the backyard, there is something magical about planting and nurturing your own food from the land.

Yes, it is true that growing your own food can come with an array of challenges including fighting mother nature's fury, battling insects that seem to destroy those beautiful leaves or even those not so cute rabbits and deer that help themselves to the fresh vegetables the minute you leave the garden. However, it seems to all come together when you pluck that first vegetable from the vine and taste the fruits of your labor.

If you're not a grower, maybe our list below will spur you on to try your hand at growing a little food of your own in the coming years. Be careful though, gardening can become quite addicting! We have listed our favorite reasons to grow your own food below, although not in any particular order, as each individual has their own unique reason why growing their food is important to them.

5 Great Reasons to Grow Your Own Food

1. **The True Fresh Food Experience**: If you have ever grown your own food, you will totally understand what we mean here. There is nothing in your local grocery store, or even the farmer's market for that matter, that can ever compare to the taste of a 'just picked' vegetable from your own garden! Period! The crunch of a pepper, the juicy explosion of a tomato in your mouth, or eating sugar snap peas right off the trellis

provides you with that indescribable taste and satisfaction that cannot be beat!

2. **Knowing What You Are Eating:** By growing your own food, you also know exactly what went into it, or more importantly, what didn't! Whether it's freshly dug potatoes, fresh picked green beans, or a few cloves of garlic going into our favorite dish, we know for a fact that they are free and clear of any harmful sprays or synthetic fertilizers. You can't always say the same for those "fresh" veggies picked up at your local supermarket. You also know that it came from your very own yard or container – and not trucked halfway across the globe.

3. **Exercise Your Own GYM Membership:** Spend a few hours outside digging, planting, or harvesting – and you know exactly what I am talking about! Gardening is one of the best ways to get a little exercise in your life, and for a specific goal – to get fresh food!! Sure, you can go to your local gym and lift a few weights and run a few laps but gardening is exercise with a purpose! Not only are you burning calories (studies have shown as much as 300 calories per

hour) but you are growing your own health food store right in your back yard. We like to call our OWG farm our own personal GYM. The GYM of course standing for 'Garden and Yard Maintenance'. The best part of our membership is that it is virtually free!

4. **Mental Health:** Fresh spring air, the warm rays of the sun beating on your back, the feel of a cool summer rain falling gently on your skin and your hands working in the warmth of sweet smelling earth are all part of the wonderful experience of gardening! Fifteen minutes spent in the garden can go a long way to erasing a stressful day at work. In fact, there are scientific studies that suggest that the soil in the ground harvests bacterium which may stimulate serotonin production, resulting in you becoming more relaxed and happier. For both of us it is an easy and completely free way to unwind from the daily grind of work and life in general. And the best part – it rewards you back with great food on the table!

5. **Family, Friends and Neighbors:** Gardening brings out the best in relationships with your

neighbors, friends and your own family. As much as we enjoy gardening we also love to share the fruits of our harvest with new and old friends alike. There seems to be an unwritten rule among gardeners to share their harvests which provides for the making of some wonderful and lasting friendships. It's also a great way to pass along knowledge and tradition. For instance, a couple of summers ago, as the oldest in our family was home from college, she spent the afternoon helping us harvest garlic. We both looked at each other and smiled as we heard her say, "This smells so good!! I can definitely see myself having a garden someday!" Those words were music to our ears as we knew then that another seed had been planted for a future generation to carry on what each of our parents passed on to us – a love of gardening!

Although growing a vegetable garden is the best way to provide large amounts of fresh food for you and your family, it, of course, requires an annual effort. After all, no matter how beautiful and productive your tomatoes, peppers and corn grow, these annual plants die off at some point each season and need replanting the following year. That is where perennial crops can really help fill in the gaps!

Growing perennial plants, bushes, and trees, such as asparagus, strawberries, blueberries, blackberries and grapes, can fill a huge void in your year-round food needs. Add in the bounty of a few fruit trees, which can bring in a variety of fresh apples, cherries, pears and more, and you just might have all you need!

Another benefit of planting these perennial crops is that, although they are incredible to eat fresh, they also are perfect for making jams, jellies, pies, cobblers and more. They are also some of the easiest crops to store and preserve. As much as I love fresh veggies from the garden, it would be hard to live without homemade apple butter, strawberry honey jam or blueberry pancakes that perennial crops bring to the table!

We have listed some of our favorite, low-maintenance perennial crops that we have added to our OWG garden, landscape and farm.

Strawberries and Blueberries

Both strawberries and blueberries are low-maintenance crops and one of the easiest to add to your landscape or even in containers. As perennials, they continue to keep producing year after year with little effort on your part.

Although there are hundreds of varieties to choose from, strawberries for the most part can be divided into two categories, June bearing (sometimes called Spring bearing) and Everbearing.

June bearing have always been our personal favorite – simply because they tend to be larger and more plump – and what most of us know as "true strawberries". We also like the fact that they come into season all at once for about 3 weeks allowing big harvests that are great for making preserves. This allows us time throughout the summer to concentrate on other crops that peak later in the year.

Everbearing varieties are an excellent choice for patio planters and small spaces. They also are perfect for people wanting to have a small supply of fresh strawberries throughout the growing year to enjoy on salads, or as a topping on yogurt, ice cream or cereal.

Blueberries on the other hand can grow on compact bushes and provide a steady crop of fruit for 20 years or more. There are three types of blueberries: large or highbush, lowbush and half-high, which is a mixture of the two. The lowbush and half high work well for us because they tend to be more "winter-hardy" which handles the varying temperatures of a central Ohio winter with ease.

You must be patient when planting blueberry bushes. They can take up to 5 years to reach their peak production level; however, they make an excellent choice for backyard gardeners because many of the varieties are compact and take up little space compared to large fruit trees or nut bushes. They are delicious when eaten fresh, great in muffins and can also be used to make syrup and jams. You can also freeze them right after picking in order to have a steady supply throughout the winter months.

Asparagus

Asparagus is different from most of the vegetable crops planted in the garden. As a perennial they can provide a good crop for 20 to 25 years for you and your family to enjoy!

Interestingly enough, asparagus plants are either male or female. The males are known to have larger and more abundant spear production, while the female varieties tend to be thinner and produce seeds in the fall for reproduction. Popular male varieties that are found in our area are Jersey Giant and Jersey Knight which make for great choices for those looking for maximum yields.

Asparagus can be started from seed or from what are called crowns – which are nothing more than the roots of 1 to 2-year-old asparagus plants. Most people prefer starting them with the crowns and not from seed to get a jump on harvesting a good crop in just a few years.

Although the harvest season is typically only a few weeks in length, the taste of fresh picked asparagus from the garden can't even be compared with what you buy in the supermarket – it is simply the best you will ever have!

Fruit Trees

There is something that is so satisfying about planting fruit trees, knowing that you are playing a part in creating a delicious and nutritious food source for you and your family for years to come. The varieties are almost endless depending on where you live apples, pears, peaches, plums, and cherries just to name a few.

Fruit trees are a valuable addition for those that are trying to be more responsible for growing their own food, and other than a little pruning from year to year, require little maintenance for the bounty of harvest that can be gained each season.

Although you can plant fruit trees in your landscape at any point of the growing season, fall is really the best time to plant. By allowing them to become established in the cooler temps of late season, the trees have a much better chance of surviving the stress of transplanting.

Whether you would like to grow your own cherry, pear, or apple trees – take care when you select your fruit trees. Make sure you select varieties that are hardy and tolerant to your growing zone. In addition, most fruit trees require a second pollinator to insure that the trees will bear fruit so be sure to read each tree label carefully to see what varieties are compatible with each other.

Grapes

Growing your own grapes can provide all types of food options. Green or purple table grapes are perfect for eating fresh and others like the Concord varieties are perfect for making juice, jams and jellies. And then, of course, if you happen to like wine, there are plenty of varieties to choose from to make a great glass of homemade vino!

Grapes are also a crop that gives a lot of options for fitting into your landscape. They can be planted and trained to grow along a fence row or made to grow up and fill an arbor that doubles as a summer shade provider. You can also plant them in the more traditional post and wire set-up that can be found at many vineyards that dot the landscape in all corners of the world.

Be forewarned, like many other perennial crops, grapes are a long-term proposition, taking anywhere from 3 to 5 years to see the first sizable harvest. The upside is that they can produce quality grapes for decades to come!   In fact, the grapes that Jim's father started in the 1970's are still producing strong!

Canning

Beyond the incredible fresh food that our garden and perennials provide, harvest time also means that canning and preserving go into full swing at the house!

If you walk into our kitchen anytime between the summer months of July and August chances are you will hear the rolling boil sounds of the water bath canner, the hum of the food saver bags being sealed, or the woosh-woosh of a pressure canner in action. To us, it's music to our ears because they represent the stocking of our home-grown grocery store.

Between what we consume fresh and preserve from the garden and farm, we supply a large majority of our home food needs throughout the year. For the most part, our grocery store visits are now concentrated on only the outer perimeter aisles...fresh fruit (what we can't or do not grow yet), milk, orange juice and meats.

What we grow fresh, can, and freeze lets us stay clear of the "middle aisles" of a grocery store where most everything is packaged and loaded with all types of preservatives. It's great to know, at any time of the year, we can head to our canning pantry for our own pasta sauce, green beans, corn, ketchup, salsa, picante, pickles, relish, ketchup, tomato juice, jams and more.

Although it's certainly true that growing and preserving your own food can save big money on grocery bills, our real goal is to know exactly where our food comes from and what is in it. Or maybe I should say to know what's not in it – like sprays, pesticides, artificial fertilizers and preservatives!

The key to having our year around healthy 'food supply' is creating a list of what we like and use throughout the year. We then plan and plant the garden based on those food preserving goals. It's actually a simple process. The key for us is to create a list of what we like most and what we use throughout the year and making sure to plan the garden and subsequent harvests so that we can meet our "food preserving" goals.

We know that we enjoy a lot of tomatoes, green beans, onions, peppers and garlic on many dishes we make throughout the year so we simply calculate out what we use of each on average in a given week/month or year and make sure we can grow accordingly.

Just as important, before we head full-bore into preserving season we do a thorough inventory of our canning cupboard and freezer to use up what we have left and to adjust what we will need to preserve to fill it back up.

Each season, we get a little better at knowing how much produce we will need to get us through the year, and fine tune the plan. For instance, we have begun to can a lot more of the items we use sparingly (relish, hot pepper rings, diced tomatoes) in more 1/2 pint jars so that we can have just the right amount on hand when needed and reduce waste.

On that note – when we freeze we have learned to make things in individual or family size portions to make the best use of space. One of our favorites to make are stir-fry packets that already have all of the vegetables cut and ready to go for a single meal portion or a large sized family meal. It makes creating fast dinners a breeze!

Plan to Can

We've figured out that the best way to maximize our effort is to plan now for what we want to eat later. It's really no different than the age-old concept of planning out your week's meals before heading to the grocery. It eliminates ending up with produce that you have no idea what to do with in late fall and not enough of the ones you need to can and freeze to feed your family. Here are some helpful tips to help **Plan to Can:**

Take stock now of what you eat and need year-round

This may sound simple but it's easy to overlook! Nothing can beat the taste of a freshly picked ear of corn, or a spring onion pulled right from the ground. But sometimes we get caught up in thinking only about the fresh and not about what you and your family eat and enjoy the most all year long. The key is to take both the fresh and year-round concepts and translate them into your garden plan, planting enough to satisfy both needs.

A great example for us is tomato juice. We both love our homemade tomato juice. It's delicious and most importantly we know exactly what goes into it, just our organic tomatoes! On average we go through a quart jar every week, meaning we need a minimum of 52 quarts canned to get us through. The result, a dedicated row planted each year for our juicing tomatoes. For many years that row netted over 70 quarts of juice!

Tomatoes, in fact, take up a large part of our garden space because we use so many tomato-based products throughout the year. Homemade pasta sauce, salsa, picante, pizza sauce and ketchup are all big hits in the house. We make a pasta dish almost weekly for a family meal and the kids can devour a jar of salsa in a single sitting. The result, 3 entire rows in our garden each year dedicated to Amish Paste and Roma like tomatoes which are great for making sauces, salsas and more.

Plant More of What You Currently Buy

This is also the time to think about what you purchase now and what you could grow, or grow more of, to preserve. We fell in love with the taste of our canned green beans the first year that we preserved them but we just didn't plant enough to store as many as we would typically eat. Since then, we have adjusted our plan and we have bumped up the number of planting rows from one single row to two double rows.

All of this planning can save big money! We have not purchased a store bought can or jar of tomato juice, salsa, picante or pasta sauce in four years. Just using a conservative estimate, that saves us nearly $700 a year on those items alone. The best part is knowing that it's home grown food with no preservatives or chemicals.

What could be better than that?

Growing for The Freezer and Freezing Smart

The same concept goes into freezing. We love to use peppers, onions, and snap peas in stir fry's and other dishes, so we make sure to plant enough to eat fresh, and preserve some by freezing for later. We also freeze a large quantity of our Cajun Belle and Jalapeno peppers to use later as quick appetizers.

When we first started out we would simply freeze them into big bags, only to find out we could never use them up quick enough before going bad. Now we freeze sliced green peppers, onion, and snap peas in the perfect dish serving size. Come winter it's a snap (no pun intended) to pull them out and throw them in whatever we are making. No waste of time or produce!

Thinking Outside of the Box with Surplus Vegetables

You also have to think outside of the proverbial box when a certain plant goes crazy and you're left with a huge surplus. A few years back we had a mammoth crop of hot peppers. We love them more than anybody, but there are only so many fresh jalapenos and habaneros you can eat in a given day without shooting flames out of your head. The solution: we decided to take the extras and dry them on low heat in the oven and in our smoker. The result? We now have some of the best homemade pepper grind, flakes and chili powder we have ever tasted. We've since cut back on the amount of peppers we grow but we make sure to include enough every year to roast a few pans for our needs.

Sadly, the majority of food products that end up on most dinner tables today have been grown with heavy doses of synthetic fertilizers, sprayed with tons of pesticides, and then are processed to contain a seemingly endless list of preservatives. It doesn't take a scientist to know that the effects on our long-term health are anything but good. In fact, all of the above have been linked to a plethora of health risks from cancer to diabetes and everything in between. Maybe it's time we all start to take charge of our own food sources and grow a little more of our own food.

There is really only one way to ever know for sure what is in your food and that is to grow it! And believe me when I say that the health benefits go far beyond just eliminating the harsh and sometimes deadly preservatives that are found in nearly all of the commercially grown and processed food today. In fact, growing your own organic-based vegetable garden covers every aspect of a healthy lifestyle from getting a dose of fresh air and sunshine (a great and NATURAL source of Vitamin D), to the exercise gained and calories burned while planting, maintaining and harvesting. But most importantly you will be putting the most nutritious, natural and fresh food into your body - home-grown produce!

Start Small

The best part of growing your own food is that you don't have to have a 100-acre farm or even a large outdoor plot to begin. Whether it's a small 10' x 10' raised row or raised bed space in your back yard, or a few simple planter boxes on a small patio, you can be well on your way to growing fresh tomatoes, peppers and more. Add in a small cold frame or windowsill growing box and you can have a fresh supply of home-grown lettuce to go along with it. And trust me when I say once you have tasted the fruits of your own labor it won't be long until you want to grow more!

As our garden and love of gardening has grown, so has our ability to provide a larger portion of the food our family consumes. Our garden's raised rows now account for the majority of the meals that end up on our table throughout the year and we don't spend every free hour we have maintaining it. On average, we spend less than 10 minutes a day in our 40' x 60' raised row/raised bed space and it provides hundreds of meals.

It seems that every year, more and more people are coming back to the art and joy of gardening. Not just because they love the feel of getting their hands in the soil but because they ultimately want to feed their families better tasting and healthier food while saving money. As food prices continue to rise, people are looking to the garden to offset the cost at the grocery store. There is no better way to feed your family than growing, cooking and preserving your own food.

Creating our new barn from two old barns

The Cardington Barn

Dad's barn during tear down - complete with 37 Chevy

The first coop at the farm

The second "mink proof" coop under construction in 2013

The completed coop

Our very first garden at the farm in 2011

A bountiful harvest from the garden

We now grow all of our potatoes in space saving crates

THE GARDEN PLAN

Each year, we develop a garden plan designed around our family's food needs. This is our 2016 plan.

PERMANENT STRAWBERRY BED

45 feet total

Green Bean - Bush Lake	(3/4) Purple Ch / Brandywine
Green Bean - Purple	(4/4) Yellow Taxi / Valencia
Cabbage - Red / Green	(8) Amish Paste
Onion	(8) Amsih Paste
	(4) Cal Wonder Green Pepper / (4) Revolution Orange Pepper
Popcorn - Strawberry	(4/4) Jalapeno / Cayenne
Popcorn - Ladyfinger	(6) Banana Peppers
Sugar Snap Peas	(4) Italian Roaster Peppers / (4) Cajun Belle Peppers
Broccoli / Cauliflower	(8) Red / Orange / Yellow Bell
Green On. / Spinach	Kale / GARLIC
Carrots / Radishes	Lettuce / GARLIC

3' WALKWAY

5' WALKWAY

3' WALKWAY

FRONT - GARDEN FENCE — 60 total feet

3' POTATO CRATE / 3' POTATO CRATE — WOOD CHIPS STORAGE

RAISED BED HERBS — FINISHED COMPOST / SOIL BINS

275 GL. RAINWATER TANK

RAISED BED HERBS — LEAF / STRAW STORAGE CRIB

3 SWEET POTATO CRATE / 3' POTATO CRATE — COMPOST STARTING BINS

GARDEN
old world farms
garden
oldworldgardenfarms.com

The recycled brick barn patio- one of our favorite farm spaces

The recycled outdoor barn kitchen

The barn doors we created from old barn flooring

With WBNS 10-TV Anchor Kristyn Hartman during her visit
to the farm for a story on OWG.

Enjoying a laugh while presenting to the Union County
Master Gardeners during their visit to the farm.
We say it often, but for us, it really is about having fun.

With Jason Miller of Weaver Barns. We have met some
wonderful people along the way - but the folks at Weaver
Barns have become like family to us as we get set to build
our "Simple House" at the farm.

Our family

Mary's mom, dad, brothers and sister

Jlm's mom, sisters and brother

chapter ten

Coming Full Circle
The Building of Our Own Permaculture

Our compost at the farm, ready to replenish the soil

When we first cleared the land it was with the intent of having our first garden together in an area that we could call our own. In no time we agreed that we also had enough room to raise chickens in the hopes of having farm fresh eggs that we could use to help feed our family. Little did we know at that exact moment, we began our adventure into developing our very own self-sustaining lifestyle.

The term permaculture became popular in the

1970's and continues to gain popularity to this day. I will not go into all of the scientific meaning behind permaculture, but I will give you our perspective of what permaculture means to not only us, but the impact that it could have on our whole world. With only a few small steps or changes that each person could and should be a part of, everyone can have a positive impact on our environment.

To us, permaculture focuses on taking care of the earth by using simple resources that are, or can be, available to you and giving back to the environment. It also means taking care of yourself and others – living a simple, yet balanced lifestyle. Lastly it means to use your resources wisely – taking only what you need and sharing what is left.

These three principles can be a huge factor in living a happy and sustainable life and we will look at each area in depth.

1. *Taking Care of the Earth*

When we talk about taking care of the earth, we aren't talking about planting trees everywhere on Arbor day and calling it quits. What we mean is that we need to protect and save the earth by making some simple changes in our daily practices. We need to use renewable resources, conserve water, build up and give back to our soil that feeds us, recycle, reuse and minimize waste products. As we built our farm, this became a very important focus for us and one that came about mostly out of necessity.

When we first built the garden we both agreed that using a rototiller was not the answer for us. For one, it would take entirely too long for the amount of garden space that we wanted to use, but also because we would not be planting in the typical garden format found in the Midwestern United States. We both grew up with families who would rope off a rectangular area and till the entire ground under, over and over again until the soil became fine. This meant that in order to plant those rows, you had to step on tilled up earth that would never harbor a seed or plant. This system allowed for weed seeds to trickle in by wind, bird, or insects. That meant countless hours of weeding for us kids and the learned perception that gardening was too much work.

If being in your garden becomes too demanding, laborious, repetitive, or just not any fun, there is probably a better way of doing it. It is time to think outside the box and not necessarily garden like Grandpa did. We don't drive cars, live in houses, or work the same jobs as they did, so why should we assume that we should have to garden like they did. Now many people find the tiller method of gardening works for them and if that is the case, by all means, use it! If it doesn't seem like excessive work for you, then keep at it. But for us, time was of the essence. We have two busy careers, 4 active children that are involved in a lot of extracurricular activities, and we knew that we needed to find a more reasonable answer. Raised row gardening became the key to our gardening success. We piled material from the earth – straw, leaves under dirt, added compost and planted our entire 20' x 60' garden in an hour. To us, that was fun!

Now came the obstacles that led us to furthering our permaculture endeavor. We had no way to water our plants. We had no running water at the farm, and in our area Mother Nature is hit or miss. Sometimes there will be a nice spring rain to nurture the crops for a few days, but typically what happens is that after you get your garden plants settled into the earth, Mother Nature seems to turn the water tap off. Watering our first garden consisted of us hauling milk jugs from home in a crate and watering each plant when needed. We knew that by next year a different solution had to be in place. So as we began to build our barn we planned for two large water tanks that would be added to the ends of the downspouts so that we could collect rainwater throughout the year. At first we only had the back half of the barn roof hooked to gutters that supplied a single tank, but surprisingly, one good, hard rain, and the 275-gallon tank was full. It was perfect for us to water not only the garden, but also for supplying water to our chickens.

And when it comes to chickens, it is hard to find a better example of how permaculture and a self-sustainable lifestyle come together than keeping your own flock of beautiful birds. If everyone had a few backyard chickens, this world would be a better place. I am not talking about roosters running around and scaring off small dogs and children, but talking about a few hens that produce the wonderful eggs that many of us enjoy in many meals and desserts. Farm fresh eggs are the best that you will ever find. Ask anyone who bakes with them and they will tell you there is no comparison in the taste and texture of their goods. And who could argue with the satisfaction that comes from knowing where the eggs came from, how fresh they are, and that you had a part of caring for these hens that made this all possible. We understand that not every place or situation will accept or allow for a few harmless birds to roam your property, but the benefits of having chickens is a prime example of applying basic permaculture principles.

Not only do chickens provide eggs for us to eat, they also provide an excellent source of nitrogen that is crucial in providing nutrients for our soil. Their manure is one of the primary ingredients in our compost pile, which in turn gets added to the soil in the growing rows of our garden. The plants flourish with this extra luscious soil, which allows for great yields. That produce is used in our kitchen to provide our family with healthy and nutritious meals. In turn, those same scraps are fed back to our chickens and end up back in our compost pile to feed the garden once again. This self-sustainable cycle gets repeated again and again.

Another benefit that chickens have in raising a garden is that they eat all sort of bugs, including many that may be harmful to your plants. As a prime example, during our first year at the farm, our property was overrun with ticks. So much that with just one step in the grass it was a near certainty that you were sure to find a tick crawling up your leg. After just one season of having our chickens roam the land, our tick population became virtually nonexistent.

Beyond the obvious sustainable methods found in nature, there are many additional ways to conserve our finite resources. Both our chicken coop and barn are made from used materials that we were able to use in a new way. As part of the permaculture design, it is important to find a new way to reuse nonrenewable resources such as pallets, crates, and even old barn flooring and wood. Our chicken coop is made from old pallets and shipping crates, our barn is made from the materials of two old barns that we tore down, and even our brick patios are created from materials that once had a different home. We had large stockpiles of excess barn wood that we did not have a specific use for and for a few months inhabited the entire garage at home. We were able to help others find the perfect barn wood for their own projects including the building of bathroom shelves, wood siding for a home office, and hardwood floors for a brand new home. We also met some great and crafty people who put the extra barn windows to use for craft shows, picture frames, and address signs.

Although we are talking about large and adventurous projects that we took on to help build our dream, there are simple things that everyone can do to help build a life towards their own permaculture design. One of the easiest ways that each and every person can be a part of a self-sustaining culture on a daily basis is to participate actively in recycling. Many of you have been doing this for years, but you would be shocked at the number of people that don't recycle at all. Drive around your neighborhood after the holidays and look at the waste left for the garbage agencies to transport to the land fill. A countless number of cardboard boxes that have been stuffed with wrapping paper, bottles, and cans and left at the curb. The most common excuse in our area is that the agencies charge you extra fee to pick up the recyclables. Within 5 miles of our home, there are 7 recycling locations that accept all sorts of items that don't even have to be sorted. I am sure that on the way to work, school or the store, most people drive by one of those locations each week. Between composting kitchen scraps and recycling our waste, our family of 4 that live at home full time will produce on average, less than one kitchen bag full of trash each week. Multiply that by each family in our community and that is a huge, yet simple, impact on our environment.

2. *Taking Care of Yourself and Others*

When most people think about taking care of themselves they immediately think about how to eat healthy and exercise more. While that is very important, when you look at taking care of yourself you must take a holistic approach to the matter. Everyone knows of that superstar who is very fit, eats well and seems to be living a dream life with fame and money. Next thing you know; we are watching a story on the evening news that they were found dead from an apparent drug overdose or an apparent suicide.   Don't assume that healthy means living what society has deemed as the American

Dream - living with more possessions and less meaning to life. A balance in life is what is important.

In order to take care of yourself you must find a healthy balance between self-care, work and leisure. The balance ratio will be different for each one of us, as our lives are unique. It is important to remember that this balance may be impacted and may need to be adjusted based on various events that happen throughout your life.

Here are some helpful strategies that we have used to help keep our lives balanced and to decrease the feeling of being overwhelmed and stressed:

Evaluate how much time you spend in each role of your life

Keep track of your daily activities on a calendar for a week to identify how much time you spend on work, self-care, leisure, and where you might be able to make realistic changes to achieve greater balance. Balance doesn't mean equal time, although in theory that would be really nice. Balance means fulfilling your obligations and creating time for the other aspects to life.

Plan your time wisely

The more hectic your lifestyle the more important it is to plan your time and activities. Before each week take time to think about the week ahead. Make a daily list of the things you want to get done and identify and prioritize the most important ones. We use a small memo pad that you can easily carry with you in a pocket or purse. As you accomplish each task, cross them off your list and take a minute to focus on your success. Whatever didn't get done that day, reassess the need and if it is still a priority or a need, add it to tomorrow's list. Seeing that item on your list day after day will motivate you to get it done.

Make sure to do what's meaningful to you.

Consider your physical, social, spiritual, emotional and intellectual needs and ensure your daily activities fulfill these. In your memo notebook write down at least one activity that you would most like to accomplish for yourself and make this as one of your priorities. 15 minutes a day of doing something for yourself will pay off in your ability to get through the rest of your day.

Be realistic in setting your goals.

While winning the lottery may be a goal for all of us, is it realistic? Although when asked what our goals are, we tend to think of long term goals. We need to break those goals down into smaller and reasonable goals that we can accomplish in a given timeframe. Five years ago if we wrote down our goal to live at the farm, we would've been lost. We knew that living at the farm was about 7-10 years down the road, but we knew we could help prepare for that goal by getting other things accomplished to help us eventually achieve the ultimate goal. That is why we also list our top 24 goals each December for the following year. We not only talk about it, we write it down and hang it on our refrigerator as a reminder to stay on track. Not all goals may be achieved that year – priorities may have changed or a different and unexpected project popped up that takes priority. The important thing is to determine what you need to do to achieve them, and act on these.

Make your days off (weekends) work for you.

Surprisingly many of us spend over twelve hours each weekend doing household chores and running errands. Although difficult, try and spread your activities out over the week. For instance, grocery shopping during non-peak hours is both faster and less stressful. We prefer to go to the store first thing in the morning when most of the world is taking their first sip of coffee. We also use time on the weekends to bond as a family, making and eating meals together, playing family games and reconnecting with friends.

Take a look at your values.

What is really important in your life? Build in the time for what is most important to you rather than acting on what you "should" do or what society says you should do. Plan at least an hour on your day off to do something you enjoy – take a walk, read a book, have tea with a friend, or even work in the garden. Whatever you choose, make sure you are the one choosing it. It not only makes you feel fulfilled; it makes the rest of the time doing activities for others more rewarding.

3. Using Your Resources Wisely

Be aware of what you consume or use, take only what you need and share the rest. When planting our garden, we establish a list of what we predict it will take to make the recipes to fill our canning cabinet each year and what amount that we like to eat fresh or freeze for later use. This involves taking inventory of what we have left in stock and guessing what a typical yield will produce. Some years we have too many vegetables to use ourselves so we give them away to family, friends, and our community through donations. We strive to use what items we have in our pantry, refrigerator or freezer before they go bad by fixing them fresh, consuming before the expiration date, or freezing the items for later use.

Accept that the shipping of items across the world may not be the best use of sustainable resources. Local produce is mostly seasonal, and there is a reason for that. Fresh strawberries are not found in December in Ohio. Consider buying or growing extra when they are in season in your local area and freezing or preserving them for use throughout the year. Although this isn't possible for all items, doing it for those that you can will help decrease fossil fuel use.

Don't just stop at foods; buy any and all local items whenever you can. For instance, instead of running to the chain discount store for a birthday card, stop by a locally owned shop and pick one up. Or better yet, make one yourself – not only is it a way to save money, it means so much more to the lucky recipient!

One of the most important concepts of this principle is accepting limits on what is truly needed, use those things wisely and getting rid of the excess. A couple of years ago we started the One a Day/365 Program. This isn't some expensive program that we ordered from a late night infomercial. We came up with this term as we decided that we needed to decrease the unnecessary and unused items in our house. Every day we would each remove one unneeded and unused item from our home by giving it away, selling it, or donating it.

Now we aren't hoarders or stepping over items just to manipulate our way through each room. In fact, I would say that we are on the more conservative side when it comes to excessive items. However, no matter the size of your apartment, condo or house, if you have rooms, you are going to fill them. Not only do you have your basic seating area, you have end tables, coffee tables, and drawers hiding behind drawers. Think about your home right now. Is there one drawer in your house that is empty? Nope, not in our house! We have coupons tucked away, envelopes, cards, pens, notepads, etc.. And if you open up your door to where you store your coffee cups. How many do you have? Do they all get used at once?

These are just a few examples of things that we paired down almost immediately when we began the decluttering experiment. However, on day 185 it began to become quite difficult. All the obvious drawers had been cleaned out and now it was time to get rid of those items that are kept in the back of a closet but at some point had a sentimental meaning at one point in our lives. For me the turning point was getting rid of the track spikes that I wore in the State Championship meet when I was a sophomore in High School. I really had no reason to keep them. They weren't going to be bronzed and placed in some trophy case somewhere, and for me, I have the memory of the day, with or without the shoes. Jim also made a tough choice that day. He had the basketball that he scored his 1,000 point with and again, he decided that it is the memory that counts, not the physical object. We turned the corner that day and really began to live with the philosophy of living with less is truly living with more.

We recently began our Simple House project to help us continue the dream of living as part of our own permaculture society. We will be using sustainable resources such as solar power, rain water collection, and will be continuing permaculture practices that make growing fruits and vegetables easier and more sustainable with reducing the work involved. This will help us produce a bigger and healthier harvest and most importantly being a part of a happier and healthier world.

chapter eleven

Creating the Farm on a Budget

Building our farm from scratch without breaking the bank

A beautiful sunrise through the grasses of our farm

It is said that necessity is the mother of all invention. When it came to the building our farm however, I think it can best be said that the budget, or better put, the lack of one, was the mother of our invention.

When we first cleared off the 3-acre field in the fall of 2010, we were starting with a completely blank slate. There were no buildings, no patio, no garden, and certainly no bushes, fruit trees or shrubs. In fact, there wasn't a single plant to be found on the land unless, of course, you count a small stand of 10 or so trees along the roadside at the front entrance. In fact, about the only thing that had shown it could grow well to that point was poison ivy – which had completely engulfed every nook, crevice and cranny of the front trees.

It would be hard enough to carve out a farm on this barren property *with* money let alone trying to do it without incurring a single penny of debt. But we were bound and determined to show that it could be done – and with a little flair to boot!

With that said, we were left with two choices to make it all happen. We could take baby steps and purchase building materials and plants as we could afford them or we could start looking anywhere and everywhere for free materials and plants to make it happen now. The choice for us was easy – the sooner the better! Before I go any further on this subject, I can't stress enough how important it was for us to have a working knowledge of what we wanted to accomplish before we ever began this entire journey.

It's not that we necessarily had all of the details and particulars worked out. It simply meant that we had a shared general vision and knew what types of materials and plants we needed and were looking for – and the farm and home we ultimately wanted to build.

So many times people ask us our "secret" to getting so much done so quickly. I really think that, more than anything else, it was that initial shared vision, that allowed us to plan and look for the salvaged materials and transplants we needed and not just start collecting everything in sight.

For us, we knew we wanted to create an "old world" feel and charm to our little farm. From the very beginning, along with our garden plans, we knew that someday we wanted to have an old-fashioned barn, brick walkways, and perhaps a patio or two of old stone or brick. We knew we wanted to plant grapes and create a small vineyard and a few fruit trees to create a tiny orchard.

We also knew we wanted a slew of ornamental grasses and drought resistant perennials that would not only add color and texture to the landscape but would be simple to maintain. That total vision kept us focused and drove us to always be on the lookout for the materials and plants that would fit the bill.

In a way, looking back now, it's somewhat scary how true that vision turned out to be and I can't help but think that having that initial plan really drove the success of the effort.

I mention this because I think all too often people that want to utilize recycled and reclaimed materials jump at everything available and then try to make it work. It's easy to fall into the "Oh, that's neat and it's free - so I'll take it and use it someday" trap. The results can really be disastrous. With that "take everything approach" it's fairly easy to end up with a small or even large-scale junk yard that is anything but attractive to your neighbors and even harder for you to manage. "I'll use it someday" is a term that can lead somewhere between a garage you can't park in and a barn full of junk – both of which contradict the living simple theory!

From the very beginning of our project, whether it was building materials or plants, we were extremely careful to try to find items that were not only free or inexpensive, but that fit our future needs or could be easily modified to do so. If not – we passed.

An Old Pile of Bricks...

Not long after we had decided to start the farm journey – our first opportunity to find free materials hit us like....well, a ton of bricks. Mary happened to be at a client's house that was in the construction business and was telling him about our plan to use reclaimed and salvaged materials at the farm. He mentioned they were getting ready in a few weeks to dig up an old brick patio to make way for a new deck and the bricks were destined for the landfill. He said he would be more than glad to dump them at the farm if we wanted them. He warned us that they would be a little muddy and that some would probably be broken, but if we were willing to clean them off and sort through them we could have them for free.

That was a lesson we learned time and time again. If we were just willing to go the extra mile we could get our hands on almost any material. It might mean cleaning off and sorting broken bricks or even fending off a large contingent of bats to get at some old barn wood. If we put in the time, the materials came at little or no cost!

Two weeks after their conversation, a large pile of bricks appeared at the top of the farm, and we were in business! We sorted through the rubble, stacking and saving the good bricks while using the broken pieces to fill in giant holes around the farm created from the ground hog dens that had taken over in the overgrown brush. It was only a few months later when we used that brick to create a beautiful patio underneath our first pergola. Grand total - $0!

When it comes to recycling, re-purposing and re-using, much of our farm's structures and hardscapes have been built at little or no cost. Among other smaller projects too numerous to mention, that list includes the chicken coop, barn, patios, compost bins, leaf silo and more. When it came to filling the barren landscape with plants, the same theory applied.

Landscaping on a Dime...

As I mentioned at the beginning of the chapter, the only plant life that existed initially on the entire 3-acre parcel was a few trees and a stronghold of poison ivy. Today, as crazy as it sounds, just five growing seasons later, we have over 1000+ perennials and grasses planted in beds all over the farm – all at little cost!

From the very beginning, we knew that, in order to fill the future beds and landscape areas we wanted to create, we were going to need a lot of plants! All it takes is one stroll through a nursery to realize that it can cost hundreds if not thousands of dollars to simply fill a single landscape bed. For us, that simply wasn't an option.

Creating A Holding Bed

Although we couldn't plan or know the final bed shapes or spaces the first few years, the one thing we could do was create a temporary home where we could divide and plant hundreds of transplants gathered from our current home, as well as the gardens of friends and families!

One of our first chores at the farm in the Spring of 2011 was to create a holding bed from a mound of dirt at the top of the hill, and another holding area in a few unused rows in our first garden. We were fortunate enough to have a fair amount of ornamental grasses and perennials growing at our suburban house, so in the spring of that year we cut back and divided as much as we could from our own plants to create some for the farm. We also never passed up the opportunity from friends, family and neighbors to take a start of anything they were willing to part.

During those first two years we transplanted hundreds of ornamental grass starts, day lilies, coral bell, lirope, lily turf and black-eyed Susan starts into the beds. We may not have had the beds created yet for their permanent home, but we knew we would need them soon enough. Better yet, they all came for free!

Another advantage of a holding bed on the property is that the plants become acclimated to the soil

– and were a breeze to then lift out of the temporary beds and re-plant when we were ready for them.

In addition to our friends, family and neighbors we were willing to use that same "work for it" principle to get some of our plants as well.

In need of some smaller variegated grasses for a new bed, we volunteered to thin out some overgrown clumps from a local business landscape. It took us about 30 minutes to dig up and divide up the large clumps and replant the smaller grasses back for them. They received some free landscaping services and we were rewarded with some beautiful ornamentals. Those grasses are now a big focal point in one of our largest beds at the farm – once again, all for free!

Buy Small – And Divide!

When it comes to perennial plants that you can't obtain for free, you can still stay within your budget if you learn to buy small and divide. Purchase those "must-have" plants in the smallest sized container you can. Let it grow for a year or two and then divide or split to have all you need as time goes by. Yes, it takes a little patience, but smaller-sized plants are MUCH less expensive in the garden stores and are actually easier to care for and get established than the larger, mature plants.

The popular specialty ornamental grasses you find now in all of the nurseries are a great example. In 2 or 5 gallon tubs - they can be as much as $30 to $50. But if you purchase the small gallon or even single starts, you can often get them for $5. In just a year or two they can be grown and split into 4 to 6 plants each at a huge savings. We have quite a few perennials at our farm that have cost us a fraction of what it would have been to purchase in large sizes and quantities – all by buying small, growing and dividing!

The re-use and repurposing of materials has become not just a way to cut costs and live more responsibly, but has evolved into a hobby and an art for us. Yes, it's true, all of the thrift and salvaging really helped us to make and build things less expensively, and sometimes far better than we could build or buy new. But, moreover, it gave us the added benefit to create history and stories into the things found in our future home and landscape.

Too many times we have become a society that throws away its past for the latest shiny object – only to realize later that the shiny object wasn't the best choice after all.

- chapter twelve -

"How Do You Two Find the Time?"

A sample of our goal list that helps us stay focused

If there is one question we are asked more often than any other, it would have to be "How do you two find the time to do all of this?"

I really don't think our story, or for that matter, this book, would be complete without explaining the answer to that question in detail.

I think for many people it might seem just a bit crazy to try balancing a work and family life, all while trying to build a farm, garden, create DIY projects and recipes and still write for the blog. But for us, we truly wouldn't have it any other way. Why? Because we love what we do! And quite simply, as we so often say in our weekly articles on the blog - *You Make Time for What You Love!*

It sounds like such a basic principle, but it's truly the heart and soul of just how Old World Garden Farms came to be. No matter if you are a winemaker, a music lover, a history buff, an avid reader or a lover of plants – you make time for what you love.

You might have 10 things going on in the office, you might have to travel here and there for your job, you might even have a second job to make ends meet, but at some point during every day or once a week you find a little time here and there to dabble in making that wine, or playing your guitar, reading a new novel, or dividing and transplanting those overgrown day lilies. You simply find a way to make time for what you love – and for us - we will always make time for the farm and blog!

Yes, we both have full time careers and an active family of four children and all of the crazy schedules and things that go along with that, but we still find a little time here and there to do what we love. As for the nuts and bolts of how we manage it all – without fail I can tell you there have been 3 methods that have helped us to make time for what we love. Our annual goal list, tiny notebooks, and something we call our " 15 minute a day philosophy" - all have been equally important!

The Annual Goals List

We had a lot of time to think about all of the things we wanted at our farm during that first winter of 2010. So many, in fact, that we didn't know where to begin. We knew that both of us wanted chickens and of course a garden but all of the other wants and must-haves became a blur as we tried to figure out what mattered the most and what was most needed. So to make a little sense of it all, we created our very first Annual Goals List – a list we still create each and every year to help give a little order to the goals that we both want for our lives and the farm.

I have to say that, to us, it is way more than just a simple list of to-do's. In fact, the process of developing it all has actually become a bonding event for both of us – helping us to realize what is most important to us as individuals, as a couple and as a family.

We follow the same process every single year.

We start by creating our own list of goals for what we feel is important for growing the farm. We limit the total to twenty-four goals – a very manageable average of two to accomplish for each month of the year. Once our list is complete, we attach a number between 1 and 24 as to the importance of each goal. Next, we sit down and read them aloud to each other. It's always amazing at this point to see how similar our goals are and how close we were to ranking the importance of them. But with that similarity comes a few goals that we each seem to write down that the other didn't - and that is where the fun all begins.

We sit down and work together to come up with the best 24 and a plan to accomplish them. It's an incredibly cathartic experience seeing what is most important to each other and compromising to come up with a plan where we both can put our heart and soul.

Then comes the most important part of all. We put the finished list up on the refrigerator. You see, for us, looking at those goals each and every day, in fact several times a day, serves as motivation and inspiration to attain the ultimate goal of a completely self-sufficient farm. And, at some point, if we haven't completed something we need to it may just keep us from going to the refrigerator to see – another helpful benefit to our waistlines!

Some might question the need to develop a list but we think it's a great way to be honest with ourselves about what really needs to be completed and what can wait for another day.   It is amazing how seeing your goals in bold print keeps your eyes and efforts focused on what needs to be done.

It has especially been beneficial for our kids to experience.   Yes, like any other teenagers would do, they poke a little fun at us when it goes up on the fridge. But as the year progresses, they see our goals getting crossed off and, more importantly, the results of the planning and work that went into them.

Without a doubt, our annual goals list has played a big role in our farm's development and success.

The 15 Minute A Day Philosophy

We are both huge believers in trying to accomplish something every day – no matter what. Even if that something is just a little part of a much larger task.

From the very beginning we started calling it "Fifteen Minutes-A-Day."

With each of us juggling the demands of careers and having four busy teenagers, time is usually the one thing that is most difficult to come by. So if we waited around for one of those rare, "all-day off, the sun is shining, the stars are aligned" kind of perfect days to get things done I'm pretty sure nothing ever would.

So instead, we decided long ago to work at least 15 minutes at something for the farm every day. It keeps things manageable, keeps them moving, and quite honestly, works for us! After all, if you are really honest with yourself, you can always squeeze in 15 minutes of your day to do something you love.

I think it all started a few years back on one of our first big projects – the building of our barn. It seemed so overwhelming in the beginning to attempt to tear down two old barns to rebuild into ours.

But little by little, each day – we worked at it.

One day it would be removing siding or floorboards from one of the old barns, another day it might be sinking a few posts for the new one. Whatever it was – we just kept at it. It was not a single day or week's accomplishment that created the finished product. Instead it was a series of 15 minutes of work here and there every single day at one single task.

Sure, there were days when we got a few extra hours in here or there...but the real key was all of those little work sessions adding up to the completed barn. The trick, as with almost anything, was simply persistence.

It really is true – just a little every day goes a long way!

The Notebook – Our 49 cent solution to daily tasks

Five minutes in the morning, five minutes at night...and a whole day of accomplishment! That is how our little notebook system works for us.

Although we rely on a digital calendar to keep track of meetings, family functions, school events and travel schedules, it is actually a simple, low-tech system that powers us to accomplish the daily tasks and goals needed for the farm. In fact, in an age of technology, time management devices, electronic calendars, alarms, reminders and task lists, I think most people are fairly shocked when they find out that our "secret" to "getting things done" is a simple, tiny little 49¢, 3 x 5" flip up spiral notebook.

For us, it actually all starts with the realization that no single large project, goal, or dream ever gets completed without a lot of little accomplishments happening to pave the way. In a lot of ways, it is a direct take off of our 15 minute-a-day philosophy. And our notebook system has really been the perfect answer to help us get those "little" things that make the whole thing work accomplished!

Every single morning, when that first cup of coffee is poured, we each take five minutes or so to write down what needs to be accomplished that day. We each keep our own little notebook list - and divvy up any tasks that are needed for the household. Everything from work needs, farm chores, grocery lists and any and all errands make the list. We attach no numbers or rank of importance to each item, instead concentrating only on what each of us has to do for the day.

Throughout the day, the notebooks are never far from our sides. Every time an item gets completed, it gets crossed off and likewise, every time a new task or chore presents itself, it gets placed on the list. It takes only seconds to do and keeps every single day right in front of us.

The small 3" x 5" size of the notebook makes it easy to keep nearby, easily fitting in a pocket, on a desk, in a computer bag or the front seat of the car. People think it's crazy but that simple act of taking a few seconds to write down a new task, or cross off a completed one keeps us connected to the day and forces us to see what else still needs accomplished.

Too often, we think of random things that need to be done at the strangest times - sharpen the mower blades, call so and so back, pick up this or that, or even fix the window that is sticking – and the notebook is a great way to get it on the schedule right then and there!

Finally, every night, we each take 5 minutes to roll through our day's list. It's easy to see for each of us what didn't get accomplished and what did.

And here might just be the most important part – instead of leaving the unfulfilled goals in their place – we turn the page and start a new list – writing out again those goals that were not accomplished yet and placing them on the next day's list. It's funny, but after a few days of re-writing a goal, it is AMAZING how much motivation we have during the day to get that goal accomplished so that we do not have to re-write it again. Writing a new list each evening also lets us start fresh and keep the list current, not having to look back over previous weeks or days to see if we missed anything.

When you write something down it tends to become embedded in your memory. It is one thing to think about what you need to do or type it into a "task list" on a computer or smart phone, but when you actually write the goal down and see it in your own writing it somehow changes it all.

And yes, those three simple methods have made our little farm all possible!

chapter thirteen

Dealing with Failures and Learning from Them!

The inside view from our homemade silo

The farm is an escape for both of us. It's not our "real job", but it is the one job that we both love no matter what. One of our pet peeves in the "real" business world has always been those times that groups hold meetings for the sake of meetings. They spend so much time thinking, meeting, and planning so hard that nothing ever happens.

I'm not sure who said it, but I have always loved the saying "Don't be a think tank – be a DO tank". The farm has always allowed us to be doers. If we had waited for the "prefect time" to build the coop, create the garden, or build the barn, we may have never gotten to enjoy any of them. And yes, we have made plenty of mistakes along the way and have had our share of setbacks and disappointments.

Failure is often looked at as a horrible thing– but I can honestly say that "The Farm" wouldn't exist as it stands today without a handful of failures.

There is one piece of advice that we give everyone who emails or asks us to tell our secret and that is it is okay to fail. In fact, if you don't fail at somethings, then you're probably not trying hard enough. After all, FAIL stands for "First Attempt In Learning", and that couldn't be more true as we began our journey to build the farm.

We don't expect our projects, our garden, or our life to be perfect 100 percent of the time. We would be happy if our successes would follow the 80/20 rule. 80% success and 20% failure. But we are real people that live real lives. We stumble, fall, and stumble again. But in between those unexpected falls, we learn and move on. There are many things that we want to accomplish and the majority of the time we don't even know where to begin. However, we don't let that stop us from moving forward and trying out each and every new adventure. We had no idea how to build a barn, but did that stop us? No! We knew that we had to build it as we envisioned it being the centerpiece of the farm, so we jumped in and attempted to figure it out, even without a clue.

The garden will have times when it certainly doesn't look "perfect". Crops will fail – weeds will grow, chickens will escape, shovels will break and trees will sometimes die. We have had plenty of failures and even more "we can do better next year" moments.

The same goes for our building projects. I can't tell you how many times something hasn't lined up or fit the way it was supposed to. That doesn't mean it can't still be fun to build or make, even if it is on the third or fourth attempt. The real key to remember is that it is more important to make the "fun" about the process and not the results. Think about it for a moment...If you could just simply throw a few seeds in the ground and thousands of perfect tomatoes grew from it without any work, would it really be fun? If you could just pound a few nails into a board and have a coop or a barn would it mean anything?

We are all faced with failure at some point in our life. In and of itself the word has such a negative connotation. But we don't see it that way. We simply could not have accomplished everything to this point if we looked at our life and the farm with a half empty point of view, and here are a couple great examples:

The Lessons of a Silo...

At some point in our farm design, we came up with the brilliant idea that every farm needed a silo! For us the silo was an excellent way to store massive amounts of leaves that we could collect each fall to store and then use throughout the entire gardening season. So we did what we always try to do, make the most of a brilliant idea. I mean at this point we may have been riding on a bit of a high from us successfully building the barn. Let's face it – if we can build that without a clue, we could certainly figure out how to build a miniature silo!

So we began the process and after about four weeks, that is when things went terribly wrong. The silo was taking shape nicely. The tall cylinder was erected and standing tall next to the barn and Jim had just spent countless number of hours trying to figure out how to make the curves for the dome. The metal was attached to the bottom half and we were in the process of trying to figure out how to cover the top. Things were looking promising until Mother Nature had different plans. A strong wind storm came through and because we had not yet secured the silo in it's final destination spot next to the barn, the wind toppled it over – right on top of our old Farm truck. Not only was the silo in disrepair, we had occurred minor damage to the door panel and side mirror of Betsy.

So, as with everything else – we thought of an alternative. We decided that a corn crib like structure would be much more manageable to build. In retrospect, the corn crib turned out to be a much better fit for the farm. We built it almost entirely from left over materials from the two old barns and it fit nicely at the back of the garden where we now store leaves and straw.

A Week of Heartbreak

Sometimes things don't come up all roses. Sometimes they don't come up at all. And sometimes things can happen at the farm that really breaks your heart. Below are some accounts that happened during one single week at the farm. In fact, it was a really tough and trying week. But, as crazy as it sounds – it's the tough weeks that make you realize how important it is to work every day at your dreams.

In March 2013, after the brutal winter that consisted of several weeks with below record temperatures and snowfall, we decided to fire up Betsy, the old farm truck. While in winter storage at the farm, it seems that field mice had decided to seek comfort and warmth inside of the glove box, under the seat, and inside of the engine compartment. To make matters worse, they decided to chew up the firewall material and wiring to make their fluffy, warm nests. After spending the better part of a day cleaning it all up we discovered the trucks two batteries finally were beyond charging and needed replaced. And then, when I went to fire up our gas generator for a little power, the cord of course, came off in my hand with the very first pull of the year! Next up, we watched one of our little ornamental pine trees shoot up in flames from a tiny spark that blew in from a nearby ornamental grass clearing fire we had set. And then finally, over the next few nights, total heartbreak occurred. For the first time since our coop was built two years prior, what we thought were raccoons, somehow found a way into what had been a secure area and claimed the life of three of our beloved chickens, including our absolute favorite "Big Mama". It was indeed a tough week at the farm. However, we had no idea how tough it would get.

Over the next several days, as we arrived at the farm, we would take a deep breath before we entered the coop. To our dismay, every day there would be a single chicken lying in the corner with her head cut off. We put out live traps, hoping to catch the culprit and the only thing we ended up catching was the same curious neighborhood cat, night after night.

We eventually began to investigate, research, and talk to everyone we knew about what could be happening. At that time, the technology of field cameras wasn't as accessible as they are today to try to gain video evidence of the unwelcomed intruder. After we lost all but 2 of our chickens, both being leghorns that were the highest fliers, we spoke to a local game warden whose theory led us to the path of the predator most likely being a mink. It made total sense after we told him the fencing dimensions and how the chickens were being left for us to find. He provided us with a mink trap which we carefully set out before leaving for the night. Sadly, I looked at the two remaining chickens and whispered good luck as I closed the door for the last time.

In the morning we were hoping to find a mink in the little box that he provided us but instead we found the remains of the last of our girls. As I looked down at the ground I held back the mountain of emotions and tears that a 'farm girl' isn't supposed to have. But I did have them, and I will always have them in some form. I was born to love animals and to this day when we have one that dies for any reason, my heart aches each time.

So the events that occurred over that period got us thinking about why we started the farm in the first place – and why we choose to garden, raise chickens, keep bees and build and work at the projects we do – even though they bring their fair share of disappointment at times.

Yes, it's true, if we had never started raising chickens we wouldn't have had the heartbreak of losing them. And if we didn't have the old farm truck we wouldn't have to worry about it getting destroyed by mice. And if the leaf silo project had never been thought of we wouldn't have lost it to a windstorm. But at the same time, we would never have accomplished a single thing. The farm simply allows us to be doers – and not just thinkers – and that makes it all worth it.

So, although our hearts became a little heavy for our chickens, and although things didn't go quite right all the time, we will keep trying and keep building and growing because the real disappointment for us would be to never try at all. The best way to put it is that we are and always will be blessed with work we love to do.

Garden Failures

Over the last few years, we have always strived to make our garden the most productive that it can be. During winter time we research various methods that may improve our garden and crop production. Last year we read about the benefits of applying red plastic around the soil for garden tomatoes and its promise of a higher yielding tomato crop. So, as we planned the garden for 2015, we decided to plant a few of our rows with the red plastic to see if it would really work.

For us, it was simply a huge disappointment! Not only was it hard to install (taking nearly 45 minutes to plant a row, a process that usually takes us about 5 minutes), but it also required the use of metal pins every 12″ or so, making it very difficult to remove later. As for the yields, they were actually way less than in our traditionally grown rows with no evidence of early ripening detected at all. Last but not least – they simply made our rows look trashy!

Our verdict – there is no need to hassle with it!

Like the growing of our tomatoes without red plastic, sometimes, it's simply better to stick with what works well! For example, we decided to plant our popcorn in a newly landscaped bed area at the top of the entrance – hoping that the ornamental look and feel of the corn stalks would add a little texture to the bed space. The top of the hill area proved to be too windy and unprotected and the popcorn crop was damaged by an early season windstorm. The resulting crop was about 15% of our normal yield – and needless to say, next year the popcorn found a home back in the friendly confines of the raised rows in our main garden!

More Disasters, But in the Kitchen

Inferno bread

There are some things that seem like such a good idea at the time, but come back later to bite you in the keister!

Last fall, after a bountiful harvest of hot Caribbean Red Peppers (comparable in heat to the Habanero), we decided to dry large pans of peppers in the oven to make some hot pepper flakes. All went well, in fact, so well that we were able to roast pan after pan over the course of a few weeks and grind them into some fantastic hot pepper flakes. They looked beautiful going in, and after 10 or 12 hours on low heat, they came out dried and perfect for grinding.

Feeling like pro's at this point, we ground up batch after batch, put away a few jars for our own use, and gave the rest out to our friends and family who love a little spice in their life.

All good so far, right??? Now, fast forward to December on a Sunday night during a family dinner which consisted of Spaghetti and Garlic bread – one of our family favorites. All 6 of us sat down to eat and within minutes into the meal, a few of the kids began to ask if we had used our "hot" spaghetti sauce instead of the regular version that we make. Now, Jim and I are both known to love hot and spicy foods, and we do indeed make a dozen or so jars of our hot pasta sauce to use when we are cooking just for us. However, I was sure I had grabbed a "normal" jar of sauce from the pantry, and like most parents, just figured the kids were just trying to find something wrong with their parent's cooking.

It wasn't until I actually saw tears coming from the eyes of our children and even in the corner of Jim's eyes, and then realized that I also had intense heat coming from my own mouth that I began to wonder what I had done to our meal. It took Jim glancing over at the counter to realize that instead of using our baking stones that we typically use when making garlic bread, he had used our non-stick baking sheets that we had used back in the fall for roasting the hot peppers. I don't think I have ever tasted hotter bread. In fact, it was downright inedible!

It seems that we both learned a valuable lesson. When you roast hot peppers on a non-stick pan, no amount of washing or cooking on them ever gets rids of the capsaicin from the peppers that makes things so hot. The melting butter and spices on the garlic bread had soaked up the hot pepper remnants and created Inferno Bread – much too hot to eat. Those pans are now dedicated to solely drying hot peppers.

Salty Salsa

There we were, early August with our harvest in full force. Every day we were bringing home crates and crates of tomatoes and peppers and something that needed to be canned or preserved. After a long day of running kids to the doctor for their annual sports physicals and shopping for school supplies for the upcoming year, I had finally made it home to begin another batch of canning. That day I set out to make our salsa. We use a ton of salsa in our house as a source for a great snack, a sauce to add to various recipes or as a topping for our tacos and fajitas.

Everything was going well until it was time to taste test the batch. I normally don't dive my spoon into the large pot until it is almost complete. So, as I was preparing the pint sized jars for canning by sterilizing them in the dishwasher, I took what I thought would be the satisfying plunge into the pot of prepared salsa. By this time, I would have most likely used 8 quarts of chopped tomatoes, dozens of peppers and onions and a variety of fresh herbs and spices.

I slowly dipped my spoon into the mixture, expecting to get a nice sampling of garden goodness. I raised it up to my lips long enough to blow it off to ensure that I wasn't going to burn my mouth, closed my eyes, and gingerly sipped all the contents off the spoon. Before I took that first bite a million thoughts ran through my head.... Hmmmmm, what was it going to taste like this year? Would I need to add a little more heat? How many jars can I get out of this big pot?

After I slowly pressed my lips against the spoon and took that first bite I knew something was terribly wrong! Within seconds, my eyes popped wide open and I immediately turned my head to the sink and spit out what was the saltiest, most disgusting batch of salsa that I have ever tasted! WHAT??? How could this happen? I have made hundreds of jars of salsa over the past several years and I had the ingredients down to a science.

I went through the whole process over and over again in my head. There is no way that this is happening, I thought. I looked into the spice cabinet and then the realization of what happened hit me! I had inadvertently used Canning Salt instead of Kosher salt in the recipe! Off to the internet I went – there had to be a solution to fix this!

Several websites recommended to counteract the salt taste with sweetness. I ran to the sugar container and began to slowly dissolve the crystals in our beautiful and pure salsa. I was heart-broken as now we had to add an ingredient that I didn't want to be a part of in our family's salsa supply. More tomatoes, more sugar – nothing helped.

When Jim came through the door that afternoon he immediately saw the mixture of horror and sadness on my face. He instantly knew that something was wrong. One taste test later, he convinced me that there was no way to return this batch to being edible. I finally agreed and the batch was thrown out.

The lesson I learned: always look at the salt source carefully before adding to a recipe. In fact, I now store our Kosher Salt in a different location than our Canning Salt. Problem solved!

Wintertime at the Farm

Our first winter at the farm was one for the record books. Very few days were bitter cold and we had minimal snowfall that year. That allowed us to build our barn during the non-gardening season and the chickens were free to roam wherever they pleased. At that time, I thought that living 20 minutes away from the farm wouldn't be so bad, even in the winter, until we had a chance to build the house and move there, which was part of the eventual plan.

That was until the following winter, when the winter of 2012 hit – and boy did it hit hard! Tons of snow, temperatures that plummeted below zero, for days upon days. We had to figure out a way to make the dangerous drive on the highway to make sure that the chicken's water was not frozen. Remember, we didn't, and still don't, have electricity at the farm. We had prepared the coop for winter by blocking the screened windows with glass and used the deep litter method to keep the coop warm enough to keep the girls happy. We added layers upon layers of straw and with the deposits of chicken manure each day added by the girls it allowed for the perfect combination to provide enough heat to keep it bearable for the hens. However, because our water container is plastic and placed off the straw, it would freeze when the temperatures were extremely low.

A nor'easter decided to barrel into our area that winter, but as an owner of animals that can't take care of themselves, there was no stopping us from making sure they were fed and had water that wasn't frozen. We were lucky enough to have an all-wheel vehicle that performed well on the snow but, like any vehicle, driving on icy roads is extremely treacherous. We warmed up the car, gathered two gallon jugs of warm water and headed out.

There was a level 2 snow emergency in place warning drivers to stay home if at all possible because the road conditions were bad. Unfortunately, we didn't have an option. We slowly began our way down the road, not reaching over 20 mph. Our trip that typically took 20 minutes ended up taking over an hour. And that is even with us following a line-up of salt trucks across the highway that helped us at least see where the road should've been if we could have seen it.

Unfortunately, the following winter mimicked the weather pattern. But this time, Jim was out of town, so I took on the sole responsibility of making the trip to tend to the chickens, this time in knee high snow! I put my boots on and made it out to the farm slowly, but safely. I was relieved when I arrived thinking that the obstacles were now behind me. I was sadly very wrong.

I exited the vehicle only to find a four-foot snow drift blocking the entrance to the barn. Feeling like I had just accomplished an insurmountable feat of arriving at the farm safely, barreling through a snow drift, although cold and inconvenient, seemed doable.

After getting snow all over my clothes, in my gloves, down the back of my neck and even in my boots I envisioned that within minutes I would be back in the heat of the car with not a worry in the world. Needless to say those minutes turned into over an hour.

As I trudged up the hill to the chicken coop, saying a few not so kind words under my breath – phrases that resembled "Why in the Hell do we have chickens", "I can't wait to move out of Ohio and never see snow again", and "It must be nice to 'work' in Charlotte and Nashville one week out of the month" (in reference to Jim's absence). I took one bitter cold deep breath of air as I finally reached the door that housed the hens. It was then that my grumbling turned into tears.

We have two slide locks on our door to the coop, one at the top, and one at the bottom. Both locks were frozen solid and I instantly knew that there was no way that my numb fingers were going to pry them open. My mind began to race for a sensible solution and no, leaving the chickens there to fend for themselves or shattering the protective window on the side to gain access were not options feasible. I shuffled through the snow, back to the barn to our make shift tool box. I found a sturdy hammer that I was hopeful would be able to loosen the lock. After a few hard swings, and stinging hands as a result of the contact, the locks loosened and I was able to gain access inside the coop. The girls were very happy to see me, immediately pecking at the snow that my boots dragged in. As I suspected the water was frozen, but I was able to switch out to the secondary water feeder. As I went to grab the eggs out of the nesting boxes I noticed that about half of them were frozen solid and had begun to crack.

Those frozen eggs ended up being just a small problem and I shrugged it off and collected them for the compost bin. As I prepared to leave, I set the frozen water feeder, feed bucket and carton of eggs on the snow packed ground outside so I could shut the coop door. Oh, if it was only that simple. I shut the door noticing that the bottom of the door was not closing enough to align to the lock. So after careful inspection of the door and opening and closing the door to see if something was blocking it, I decided that I would just lock the top one. That is when bad became worse. The top lock wasn't aligning either! The slider was about 1/8 of an inch lower than the hole that it was to slide in. Now if Jim was here, he would use his strength to raise the door up slightly and the problem would be solved. I just don't have the strength on a normal day, let alone a day that I was bitter cold.

I tried for several minutes to lift the handle with all my might, hoping that I could just get the slightest bit of lift on the door. No luck! Over and over again I tried. The frustration turned into pleading and talking to the door, and eventually into tears. I returned to the barn to collect myself. I knew I could do this – I had no option! I was there by myself and Jim was several states away. As I meandered around the barn thinking out loud to whatever creature was hiding in the corner to listen, I remembered how Jim and I lifted some of those heavy beams during the barn building process using the theory of levers. I grabbed a shovel and a block of wood and headed back to the coop with a plan. I placed the block of wood close to the entry door, the shovel resting on the top of the block with the blade of the shovel under the bottom of the door and the handle facing towards the barn. Once in place, I stood on the handle which made the blade lift the door enough so that I could slide the lock in place. SUCCESS!!! I was elated but frozen, but thankfully at that point I couldn't feel a thing.

Lesson learned: Stay calm and use the knowledge that you have stored to solve the problem.

Feeding Bambi

Although the farm is located in the country with woods and waters within yards of the property we have always been fortunate with cohabitating with the local wildlife without much of a problem. Yes, we have had our bout with Groundhogs living near and around the vineyard, but besides one grapevine that is next to the summer condo of Mr. Groundhog, we have had little damage.

Many people ask us how we deal with the bunnies and deer that would typically inhabit a location like ours. Honestly, we have only seen one rabbit since we initially mowed off the property. Our thoughts on the reason are two-fold. When we originally cleared the land there was little to no protection for bunnies to live safely at all. But more importantly, there are rumors that coyotes are nearby that greatly diminish the bunny population.

As for deer – well, we see deer tracks all the time at the farm. Whether it has just rained and you can spot the tracks in the mud, or the trails that you can find circling the farm in the middle of a snowy winter day, we definitely have several deer that visit our farm daily. Yes, we have a fence around our garden area, however it is purely for aesthetics as any deer could easily jump the 3 rung fence and if they were smart enough, they could enter at one of the open entrances to the garden. But we honestly don't have that problem. Our theory is that the deer have so much to eat around the farm including the vegetation in the fields next to us that they aren't searching for excess food sources. Well, at least we didn't think so....

I can remember that summer day perfectly. It was a Friday in mid-July and our crops of green and purple beans were coming on strong. As we strolled through the garden at the end of a day when we had just enough time to complete a few basic chores, we contemplated if we should pick the ripe purple beans, as they were the perfect size for a first picking before we headed home. We decided that since the following day was Saturday, that we would have plenty of time to come out in the morning and pick the beans. We happily drove home, discussing how nice it would be to eat fresh beans the next night at dinner. We could hardly wait to get out the canning jars from the pantry and dust off the pressure canner. Canning season was about to begin!

We gathered the harvest baskets and headed out to the farm the next morning – so early that the dew covered our shoes as we walked excitedly up to the garden. As we approached, we stopped and paused about how beautiful everything looked at this time of the year. The foliage was large and vibrant, the green tomatoes were starting to show signs that ripening was just around the corner, and the spring beds were full of crops waiting to be harvested.

With our baskets in hand we proceed to the purple bean row to collect the fruits of our bounty and then it hit us.... WAIT – What in the world happened?? Within 12 hours our abundant row of the perfect purple beans had turned into a mowed off row of stems and a few leaves. Yes...the deer had listened to our plan and decided to act before we did. They didn't touch anything else in the garden, just that row. We ended up with one small saucepan full of beans that we thoroughly enjoyed that evening, of course, longing for a second helping.

Lesson learned – Don't tell the deer when you plan to harvest – even if you think they can't hear you, they can!

Onion row seeded with cover crop

When I was strolling through a local nursery, in

late fall looking for garlic to plant, I noticed a bag of onion sets. I had never planted onions in the fall, and was baffled to discover that just like garlic, you could plant onions in October for an early crop to be harvested in the summer.

I gave it a try and I have never been happier with my full sized onions. They were plump, easy to harvest, and didn't require planting in the busy spring gardening season. That next fall we couldn't find any onion sets at the nursery and we just got too busy and forgot to order any from a seed catalog company. Fast forward to the third fall at the farm. I was bound and determined that we would have those beautiful onions once again.

I was lucky enough to have found them and a couple of days after Jim and I planted the garlic, I headed out to plant the onions. I raked over the soil from the remnants of the summer crop that had been planted in that row, added a little compost from the bin, and dug my trenches for planting. One by one the onions were scattered down the line and then covered up with the soil and compost mixture. I was elated! We had two long rows of garlic and now a triple planted row of onions that would be ours in the spring. I felt so ahead of the game.

A few days later, Jim headed out to work at the farm and get the end-of-the-season garden chores done while I had to work late. He cleaned up the potato crates, removed all the remaining stake-a-cages from the garden area, and began to prepare the garden for seeding of the cover crop. This required him to rake out any straw, leaves, stems and fallen produce out of our raised rows, except the ones that the garlic and onions occupied. He would follow that up by planting winter rye in the vacant rows. This yearly process allows us to replenish the soil with nitrogen rich nutrients which are so important for next year's garden.

In a few days after sowing the annual rye, you will find burgundy colored sprouts poking up through the soil. This indicates that the seeds are beginning to germinate. It only takes a couple of weeks to see that luscious green manure, cover-crop being formed.

A couple of weeks after planting, Jim and I both went into the garden to check on the status of the annual rye's growth. It was beautiful.....all but two rows had various levels of germination occurring and then it hit me! WAIT!!! This year we had increased our garlic to acquire two full raised rows and the onions were planted in the third row. Jim's face turned a little flush as he turned to me and realized what had happened. In his glory of planting what normally is a huge contributor to the ongoing success of our garden, he forgot that I had planted onions and seeded those rows with the cover crop as well. Unfortunately, the seeds had already sprouted - and at this point it was either turn the soil over and lose both the cover crop and the onions, or allow the cover crop to take over and replant the onions in the spring. Needless to say, the cover crop won out and I am still waiting for my fall to spring onion crop again this year.

Lesson learned: We now use our garden stakes as markers to indicate which rows are ready to be covered with annual rye. As each row is planted with a cover crop - we simply turn the garden markers around to indicate the row is ready for Winter.

Mother Natures' late freeze

May 15th is the date that we generally use as the guideline in determining when it is safe to plant our summer garden. We watch the long term forecast for a few weeks leading up to planting day just to make sure we are in the clear to proceed. The chief meteorologist at a local television station ensured us that it was safe to plant on May 15th, and from every indication from the extended forecast we agreed. We actually planted our garden on May 13th – taking a big two day, jump-start risk. We cruised past May 15th without a hitch, and in fact it wasn't until May 29th arrived that we became worried.

The sky was as clear as pure blue water with not a cloud in sight. It was a beautiful spring day in central Ohio, but clear skies are not good when a cold front is passing through – at least not for a gardener. All predictions were focused on the weather teetering around 34 degrees. For us, that was too close to a freeze to take a chance on losing our newly planted vegetables. The temperature out at the farm is usually a few degrees cooler than at our in town temperature at the house. There are lots of open fields and valleys that can draw in the cool and moist air.

With over 150 plants in place we began to scramble to find enough items to cover each and every one. We had a total of 30 buckets, pots, and planters that we could use for cover, but then what? We bounced idea after idea off each other and finally came up with the idea of brown paper lunch bags being our best and only solution. We scurried to the store, found extra-large size lunch bags and began working. After just a few minutes of carefully covering up our first few rows of delicate plants, we realized that the bags would blow or topple over at the slightest breeze. Ughhhh!

We tried to put rocks at the base of each bag which didn't work at all and then we recalled that we had purchased landscape spikes last year for our watermelon patch. We quickly ran to the barn and dug through our tack room and found a container full of used "U" shaped spikes. One on the front side of the bag and one on the back did the trick.

An hour later, after doing all we could to save our vegetable plants, we timidly drove home. That next morning we were up way before the sun, sick to our stomachs about what we might find once we returned to the farm. As we pulled down the long, rocky drive, we immediately noticed a few brown paper bags streamed across the back of the property from the entrance to the garden all the way across the front of the coop. As we made our way down the curve of the driveway, we both gasped as we were faced with 30 sangria pepper plants that were wilted from the frost. We didn't even think about covering those up in our haste to save the vegetable garden.

Before the car was placed in park, we jumped out and hurried to the garden. Some of the brown paper bags were still intact and firmly secured in place. Others were wet and had fallen over, and others were now part of our landscape in and around the garden. The damage assessment had begun.

We lost about 1/3 of our vegetable plants and all of our planted ornamental pepper by the driveway. Luckily we had grown all of Sangria plants from our own seed, and as always we over predicted what we might need. Luckily, we had extra on hand. We also had a few leftover heirloom tomato and pepper plants, but in order to fill the void we were going to have to go without or purchase replacement plants.

Lesson learned: No matter how much you prepare and plan – Mother Nature will always have the final say.

Through the entire building of the farm we have learned that every day, every week, and every moment we spend at the farm is important. Sometimes it is because we accomplished something great – other times it is because we learned a valuable life lesson. The key is to keep at it.

Another one of my favorite quotes comes from Albert Einstein, when he simply stated, "you have never failed until you stop trying". That's the way we feel about our little farm and garden. It's a never-give-up proposition for us now and always.

chapter fourteen

The People We Met Along the Way

We have met some interesting characters along the way

One of the biggest rewards in the process of building the farm and establishing the blog has been the ability to meet people from all over the world. Through emails, we have enjoyed hearing the stories from each and every one of you about fond memories of growing a garden or about living in a time that seemed so much simpler. We have also enjoyed spending time with those individuals who have visited the farm, either from the classes that we have instructed or through a mere stop as they drove by the farm. We have had the pleasure to establish long lasting relationships with several people who we would probably have never met all because of our farm. We feel very fortunate to have this opportunity to meet others and below are just a few examples of those who have left a lasting impression along the way.

Bob the Tool Guy

If it wasn't for Bob, the farm wouldn't be standing as it does today. From day one we knew that we needed help obtaining the equipment to complete massive projects to begin the farm. We wanted to use local help, so we contacted Bob at his equipment rental business. He has been a part of our story from the beginning.

We first met Bob on the day we rented the brush cutter to clear the land. Since then he has helped us pick out the appropriate piece of equipment that would best meet our needs for each project.

Our first summer at the farm we had not yet purchased our tractor and we knew that our push behind mower at the house would never be able to do the trick. We immediately contacted Bob to inquire about a zero turn mower that would be tough enough to handle the rough lawn that basically consisted of small twigs, weeds, and a ton of groundhog holes. About every two weeks we would reserve the mower and head to his shop to not only pick up the equipment, but also to have a small town friendly conversation with him as he stood behind the counter.

Bob finally asked about our seemingly never ending list of projects and rentals when we decided to rent a Bobcat with an auger as a way for us to dig holes for posts, a mini track hoe to move countless numbers of rock from the quarry and a generator and nail gun in order to secure the boards on the barn. We shared with him our story, how we wanted to create our own place from used and recycled materials, all in the mean-time making sure it was aesthetically pleasing to the eye. He quickly became interested in our projects because little did we know he drove by our property every day both to and from work. He then began to monitor our progress on a daily basis during his road trips and even stopped by a few times to lend a hand with the equipment. He was even brave enough to take a bite out of some of our hottest peppers!

Although our paths don't cross as frequently these days, with the need for machinery at a minimum for now, we always wave and smile as we see him drive home from a long day's work and we will always be thankful for his help and guidance in helping us begin the farm project.

Barn People

After the excruciating summer of tearing down two barns to build our own and the following winter when our OWG barn became a reality, we realized that we had excess barn wood that we no longer had a need for, nor the room to store for future projects. We decided that we had to clear out the wood, and we both knew that the only way to do this was to find others that could use it for their own projects. We used Craigslist and local social media outlets to alert others that we were willing to part with the wood and over the next few months we met hundreds of people who we spent hours with discussing possible and planned projects, some of which we will discuss here.

The Strength and Conditioning Coach at a major university arrived at the farm describing how he would use the wood as wall covering in a new office for his wife. Then there was a couple in their mid-70's that just built a house and had dreams of using old barn wood as shelving in their master bathroom. We also met a wonderful young couple that wanted the wood to build their own dining room table and when they left, loaded up a small, hatchback car that had wood sticking out of every window!

But the best of all was when Jim went out to the farm to meet a woman who called him looking for wood to restore an old farm house she had recently purchased. As Jim waited at the bottom of the hill, a brand new, decked out pickup truck approached the driveway and slowly creeped down the descending hill to the barn. As Jim walked out to meet her, a petite young lady jumped down from the high seat of the truck with flowing blond hair and aviator sunglasses on to protect her eyes. After discussing what the wood was going to be used for and how much she would need, as typical, the conversation quickly shifted to the subject on how the farm was built. Jim explained that she could read more about it on our blog, and she quickly became interested and began asking questions on how she could start her own blog about the house renovations that she and her boyfriend would be completing. She asked a lot of great questions and asked if he minded if she made another visit later in the week to show her boyfriend our barn. Jim agreed and before she left the farm, she fully introduced herself giving him both her first and last name along with her boyfriend's name in anticipation of next week's scheduled visit. Before she even pulled out of the drive to head home, Jim called me to confirm his suspicion.

Jim expressed to me that he had recognized this woman's name and wanted me to look it up to see if this indeed was who he thought it was. After a couple clicks on the internet, I was able to verify that it actually was indeed the recent ex-girlfriend of a very famous pop star! We couldn't believe that she had just been to our farm when just months before she was walking the red carpet and living a life that was so distant from life in Central Ohio. She had family roots in the area and dreamed of living a simpler life as well. On that next meeting, we never mentioned to her that we knew of her past life of fame, and just like we would do for anyone else that we meet, we helped her and her new boyfriend begin their own blog about their journey to restore a beautiful farm house.

The Bee Guys – Michael and Barry

When we decided to dive into bees, we knew that we needed to partner ourselves with some knowledgeable individuals if we were going to be able to pull this feat off. We already spoke about Mike, our classroom teacher and mentor that gave us the courage to give beekeeping a try. His passion, friendliness and pure love for beekeeping made us feel at ease (well at least as much ease as you can have when dealing with bees) and just knowing that he was someone we could call in a time of need, provided us with the comfort to proceed.

We ended up ordering our beehive and queen from a local beekeeper Barry. He is known throughout the community as the Bee Man. We ordered the queen and hive over the phone so we had no idea what we were going to be in for once we arrived to pick them up. There were several active hives placed right next to the main drive that led to his shop and barn. I was a little intimidated as I stepped out of the car as the bees were buzzing around me, but I remembered what Mike had taught us – just say calm.

As we entered the barn we were approached by Barry – a tall, calm, older man. He confirmed our order, and, within minutes, handed us a box full of thousands of bees, humming the same tune. We took a deep breath and began with our questions. Barry was so kind and patient with us and our million questions, which I am sure he thought would never end. As we headed down the drive back home, the excitement of becoming bee keepers was coupled with the nervousness of following correct protocol.

Over the next couple of days and weeks we called both Mike and Barry to help guide us through our uncertainties, but we also discovered a longtime friend of ours was an experienced bee keeper as well. We actually ended up at Fred's house to purchase some old metal roofing for a project unknowingly through him via a Craigslist advertisement. We met him at his farm and ended up spending most of the time talking about his bees and experiences – all the way from using local queens to how to split a hive. He has offered to come to the farm to help guide us, and when the time comes to split a hive, his presence will be more than welcome!

Pergola Customers

It's a bit funny how it all started. I would love to tell you it was a grand business scheme complete with well thought out ideas, a marketing plan, and great advertising. A grand plan to build a business that would allow our farm to earn an income and create a more self-sufficient farm and life at a quicker rate.

It was, however, all by chance. You see, after clearing the land for the first time and putting in the raised bed garden, we sat in lawn chairs in the upper northwest corner of the "farm" and took in the view. While sitting, I simply said, "Wouldn't it be nice to have a nice place to sit and enjoy the garden and look out towards the (not yet built) barn and farm"? You see, we had no place to sit while we were there. The only structures that were on the farm at that time were the original chicken coop and the garden. When we were tired or needed a break, our choice was to sit on the not-so-smooth lawn or sit in the car.

After discussing our options and vision, we both decided that we liked the look of a pergola over other choices of garden structures, like a gazebo or canopy. The rustic and beautiful lines of a pergola just fit the theme of what we wanted our Old World Garden Farm to be about. Over the course of the next few weeks we looked everywhere to buy our dream pergola. The problem was, we couldn't find one we liked. We seemed to have two choices; a flimsy metal canopy that came with a not-so flimsy price at the local hardware store or the ultra-expensive wood kits on the markets that required the equivalent of a house payment. So we decided on a third option, design an old world pergola and build it ourselves.

With no power still at the farm, and much like our chicken coop, we built our farm pergola in the driveway of our suburban neighborhood. We cut our own pattern for the edges from a piece of cardboard until we settled on the curve cut that we liked, then proceeded to cut out the purlins with an old jigsaw that we had in the garage. Looking back now, I laugh thinking how long it took to cut those boards, having to stop every 15 minutes just so the jigsaw would stop smoking from overheating. We cut every curve and notch by hand, even cleaning out the notches with a hand chisel to get "just the right look". At the end of a couple long days, there she stood, our "old world" garden pergola – an all-wood, all-natural, hand-built pergola erected in our driveway. We celebrated by heading out to a local dining establishment for a celebratory beverage and meal.

And then it happened, my phone rang, and our little business started. The call was from one of the neighbors down the street who we knew through the local school. They had just driven by our driveway while we were at dinner and the pergola caught their eye. She innocently asked where we had purchased it because like us, she had been looking for a "real wood" pergola. We laughed and said we looked too, and finally had just built one. Before we both knew it, we agreed to build another one for them. We built that one in the driveway too and during the process a note appeared on the half-built pergola asking if we would build another....and then another. That year, in just a few months we built and sold many pergolas and met so many incredible people along the way.

Beyond getting to meet so many spectacular people – one of the most rewarding aspects of building our pergolas is knowing that they become a special place for people from all over to enjoy their own backyard space. I am always amazed at the creativity of people and how they can take something and make it completely their own. Although the basics of how we build our wooden pergolas are the same, each and every one looks completely different once someone takes it into their own space and makes it theirs.

We received an email from one such couple that truly blew us away with the space they created. Robin and her husband contacted us back in the early summer after building a patio from reclaimed brick, and wanted an outdoor pergola structure to go over it. So, over the next few weeks, like we so often do, we traded emails and pictures and worked our way through the design and dimensions. It ended up being a fairly large pergola, 16' x 14' with 12' posts to be sunk in the ground. On a sunny weekend in early July, they came down and picked up their custom made pergola kit. What they did with it from there is simply amazing. They built themselves their own outdoor paradise, complete with curtains, lights, tables and chairs.

We really are amazed when we think about where all of the pergolas that we designed and built have ended up. They have been installed on the top of a 40-foot deck overlooking a small forest, on top of a loft in the middle of a large metropolis city, and in backyards across six different states. We never get tired of getting pictures back from those that have purchased them, telling us how they have "made it their own". We love the stories of our newly made friends enjoying their morning coffee outside, having an outdoor dinner, or enjoying a glass of wine at night under the stars. It makes us happy to see others enjoying their own "little slice of heaven" – just like we enjoy ours at our farm.

Brewery tables

The owners of a brew pub had read one of our articles about our little farm and how we built our rustic trestle table to fit inside our barn. They contacted us and asked if we would build matching ones for their new business that was set to open in a few weeks. We met with them to gather what they exactly wanted and how our tables would fit in with their new adventure.

This family had lived the life of a typical middle American family, both parents working full time and raising their children. As retirement age came closer, they knew it was time to get into their own business and out of main stream America. The family worked together and began this adventure in preparation to living their own dream. We were honored that they asked us to build their tables for them just by reading our blog. Our very own farm trestle tables were delivered and installed a few weeks later at that local pub located in the Columbus, Ohio area. It really is an amazing feeling to think that each and every day people are sitting down and enjoying time spent with friends at the tables we built from old barn wood at the farm.

Wine Rack Friends

Building many of our projects in our driveway at our current house has allowed us to meet neighbors walking by and people driving slowly as they pass the house to see what we are building. Besides the pergolas, we have built several tables, desks, barn doors, headboards, and our most favorite, the wine racks.

We had old rough sawn barn wood left over from a recent project, so we decided to build ourselves a custom made wine rack. And yes, as you can imagine, within a few weeks, it sold. We continued to build a few more, mostly to get rid of the excess wood in our attempt to clean out the garage once again. With an extra wine rack built, we decided we would put a "for sale" sign on it in the driveway before we left that afternoon for the farm. Within a few hours, we received a phone call from someone who definitely wanted it. In fact, he wanted it so much that he moved it out of sight so that way no other one passing by either in a vehicle or on foot could see it.

We were excited that this wine rack was

going to go to someone who wanted it so badly. We hadn't arrived home yet when the second phone call came in from the same number. A sad voice came on the phone sounding very disappointed. He had gone home to measure the space where the wine rack would be positioned, and it was 4 inches too long. He apologized immensely and offered to go return the rack to a more visible location in our driveway for others to see.

We laughed, because moving the wine rack would have been something that we would have done, and we declined his gracious offer. Luckily we were able to inform him that we were in the middle of building a slightly smaller rack, and if he would like to come the next day, we could show him the work in progress. He jumped at the opportunity so we set up a time to meet.

Needless to say, we met Joe and his wife Julie the next day and instantly became friends. They are quite a bit younger than us, but we both share the same passion to live a simple, yet fulfilling lifestyle. We have enjoyed their company over several evenings out and even with each other during the holidays. We consider ourselves very fortunate to have met such an energetic and vibrant couple who we hope to call friends for many years to come.

Our Friends from The Website

Of course, the greatest people that we come into contact with every day are those that contact us through our website each and every day of the year. From the 91-year-old man who loved our straw bale gardens, because although he is slowing down, we inspired him to use this method to continue his love of gardening, to the young couple that followed our raised row gardens completely to turn their front yard into a food yard.

We have met so many of you through our gardening and canning classes, from speaking engagements, and just through the power of written communication via email. We enjoy hearing stories of what worked, what didn't work and what your plans are for the upcoming year. As much as you tell us that we inspire you, we can't thank you enough for what you have done for us. When times get tough on the farm through mishaps, tragedies, and interactions with others that threaten the safety and integrity of our farm, you are the ones that stood by our side and encouraged us to move on. The outpouring of support and love that you share mean the world to us and made us realize that we do this for a reason – to build a network of those people who believe in building a better and more simple life.

We now have subscribers from over 223 countries and although we can't always help the individual living in the desert to grow tomatoes, we are connecting thousands of individuals to share the love of cooking, canning and a living DIY lifestyle.

We owe a huge thank you to all those who supported our Kickstarter campaign that allowed our dream to write this book to become a reality. In ten short days, you came together and believed that what we do makes a difference for not only you but others. We thank you from the bottom of our hearts and each and every one of you, or a person that you designated, are listed in the Appendix of this book.

chapter fifteen

The Future

Building our Home at The Farm

The next big project at the farm - The Simple House

We would have to say that the next big project at the farm is the building of our Simple House. No, we are not talking about a multimillion dollar home with 10,000 square feet of living space. What we are planning to build is what we would call our dream home – a simple house that meets the needs of our family.

The main goals for the house are fairly straightforward: design and build as much as possible on our own at minimal cost and develop an energy-efficient, low maintenance home that utilizes only the space we need. In short it will be a simple home that allows us to live and enjoy the farm now and forever.

How small is too small? The disadvantages of a "Tiny Home" concept

Although the "Tiny Home" concept seems to be all of the rage right now, the reality is that for a lot of people, including us, it simply wouldn't work long-term. It might be perfect for a young individual or a couple starting out, but perhaps not for two people who want to create a space to retire. I don't think either of us want to spend the later years of our life climbing up a folding ladder into a loft bed each evening or pulling out a 2′ kitchen table to have our breakfast on with a grandchild.

So that is where it all begins for us in the design phase, to truly think about what space we need to live comfortably and what that space should look like.

First and foremost, we knew we did not want a big floor plan. The whole point of this project is to create a smaller space, to live with less "stuff", including the unnecessary junk that fills up unused space in homes and depletes your wallet at the same time. A smaller home has tremendous short and long-term advantages that fit perfectly into our long term plans. It is less expensive to build now and way less expensive to heat, cool and maintain in the future. So the real question became for us, how small can we make it to take advantage of all of those savings without feeling as though we were living our life in a tiny home.

Eliminating underutilized and useless rooms...

For starters, we will completely eliminate the rooms we do not use in our current home. For us, that includes the basement, a living room, dining room and a growing number of spare bedrooms as our kids head to college and beyond. Our current dining room and the living room have essentially become what amounts to an unused show room filled with furniture, decor and "stuff" that we look at, but rarely ever use! The same goes for our basement and many of the 2nd floor bedrooms. By eliminating both of those, we take out the need for any steps in the future, which is a huge key to getting around when our legs might not quite be what they are now.

Making the best of the space we do use...

The simple fact is that if you really want to downsize, you DO have to make cuts somewhere in livable space. For us, we chose to eliminate those we don't use at all – like our current living room, dining room and unused bedrooms. In addition, we cut down on room sizes that seem to eat up a lot of unused space for no reason at all – like bedrooms. Take for instance most of today's master bedroom plans that create "sitting areas and wide open spaces". For us, we just wouldn't use them, so we eliminated that space from our plan.

At a whopping 1,056 square feet of main floor living space, and an additional 200 or so square feet of loft space, our floor plan doesn't exactly exude "castle-like" dimensions. But by planning out the space we have to fit our needs, we feel like it is more than enough to do everything we could ever want without breaking the bank or sacrificing realistic comfort.

The Kitchen / Living Area

We knew more than anything else we wanted a big combined space for the kitchen and living area for The Simple House.

Our current home's set-up of a large combined kitchen and family room space has worked really well for us and it is where we spend nearly all of our waking hours. It is where we prepare and eat our meals, talk, read, visit and discuss all of life's trials and tribulations. It is in essence, the epicenter of life. The new plan will allow us to make full use of that.

In reality, we will actually gain space in that area

– going from our current home's set-up of 16' wide x 34' long family room / kitchen area (544 sq. feet), to the Simple House design which will be 24' wide x 30' long (720 sq. feet). There are also a lot of windows to add to the openness, including a double set of glass doors that will open from the living space out onto the porch that overlooks the farm below.

The kitchen and living space are completely joined and a part of each other so that we can talk, work in the kitchen and visit with guests, all without feeling cramped. We will add a large prep island to the kitchen area and small 3' x 5' kitchen table as well which will give us plenty of room to enjoy meals and company. We then can take advantage of the large open space of the two rooms to allow for set-up of additional tables, if ever needed, for larger gatherings.

This set-up completely eliminates two wasted rooms of our current home our living room and dining room but still allows us the option for a huge space, if needed, to entertain. Less upkeep, less to heat and cool and of course, less cost to build!

Eliminating Space Challenging Doors...

One of the biggest challenges of a smaller home is what to do with doors. If they swing out, they can block the hallway. If they swing in, they can eat up floor space in the smaller rooms. So we simply eliminated them and replaced the interior openings with sliding barn doors and pocket doors.

Not only do we think they will fit the farm and house theme perfectly, the large openings to our bedroom and bathroom will be more than wide enough to accommodate handicap accessibility, if ever needed. The sliding doors can also easily be converted to be push button operated, if ever necessary.

The Back of the House – Bedroom / Bathroom / Laundry Room and Mechanical Room

The back of the house plan is an extremely simple design with a single hallway that leads off of the kitchen and sliding barn door access to the bedroom, bathroom and laundry room. We have also included a space-saving pocket door design to enter the mechanical / storage room area at the back of the house.

The bathroom will have a very large walk in shower which will also be handicap accessible. We considered installing the ever popular double sink, however, we realize it is simply unnecessary. We can then use that space for a small closet or storage rack for linens and bathroom supplies.

The laundry room will have space for the washer/dryer and a much-needed utility sink, along with a space for an upright freezer. That is a must for us for storing goods from the garden! At the very back of the house we added on a small utility and mechanical room to keep the main floor plan open. This area will house the essentials for heating the house and provide adequate space for storing our homemade canned goods.

The loft space will be used as an extra bedroom / office space. We will also have built in knee wall storage down both sides of the angled walls. This will provide additional storage space for those items that are necessary, but used less frequently.

Measuring a mere 14' x 10', the master bedroom may seem small to most but for us it fits the bill. We really don't need massive unused space in the room and it is more than large enough to accommodate any size bed. We still have enough room for a couple of built-in closets, and will utilize the back of the steps for additional closet space.

To add to a more open feel to the room, we will have a double set of French doors that open out onto the porch overlooking the entire farm below. We can only imagine what it will be like to walk out those double doors and sit and have our first cup of coffee.

Although building the house and moving to the farm is the next big project for us personally, we have many more goals that we want to accomplish in the future. Our love of gardening and living a simple life have spurred on our desire to share this information through our website articles and most recently through personal speaking engagements. We will continue to experiment with various ideas with the goal to make gardening easier and pass along the results to our followers.

Moving to and Promoting the Any Age Anywhere Garden

Why the name? Because it's truly a great way for anyone, of any age, living anywhere, to grow some, most, or nearly all of their family's food. Even when space is limited!

As much as we talk about the beauty, simplicity, and ease of raised row gardening, we realize that not everyone has the room or ability to grow using that system. We receive emails from all over the world asking for alternative gardening methods for those with small yards, patios, or others that might have trouble turning the soil over or bending down to tend rows of crops.

Over the last few years, in addition to the main garden at the farm, we experimented on a small scale with a few traditional container gardens. We then added in our own methods that we use in our standard garden to see what we could create. The goal was simple. Design an attractive, inexpensive and functional container garden that anyone of any age could plant. It needed to be simple to create, maintain and harvest and conserve on space. It also, of course, had to produce enough that you could grow a significant amount of food!

Last year, we trialed tomato bucket containers. We built wooden frames with scrap lumber that went over the top of 5 gallon buckets and nursery containers. We then attached a 4' high x 16" wide wire frame to the inside of the newly constructed wooden box for a built-in, heavy-duty trellis. It was a spin-off of the Stake-A-Cage that we use in our main garden and it worked incredible and only for a minimal cost.

The higher level bucket allowed for easy watering and maintenance. By screwing in the trellis to the box it provided a perfect support for the tomato that was easy to reach and tie up the plant as it grew. The bucket provided more than enough room to establish a deep and complete root system – and the cover not only made the planter attractive, but helped to insulate the plant's base from harsh winds and helped to conserve water. It also made harvesting a breeze.

Best of all it all but eliminated weeding and ground pests like slugs. It also stopped potential damage from voles, moles and rabbits – a problem that we get asked about every day! And with the compact space it even made it easy to protect from raccoon and deer. The same holds true for our potato crates.

After the success of our first few containers at the farm we asked ourselves why not design an entire garden around this concept? After all it can be built anywhere, a patio, a small backyard or even in the middle of a garden.

The OWG 16' x 16' Trial Garden

We have decided that we will be using a 16' x 16' "garden" space to trial the Any Age Anywhere garden, using the buckets for planters. We then will fill in the edges with simple raised beds for salads, potatoes and greens. The best part of this plan is that anyone can adapt the dimensions to fit the space that you have. For instance, you can decrease the amount of containers that you have to meet your growing needs. And on the contrary, you can increase the size if you are planning to produce maximum amounts for a community garden or a co-operative group. What you have is a functional and easy to maintain garden that can produce goods almost anywhere. This garden design can work in almost any application. From community gardens to companies who wish to use unused space to provide a garden area for their employees.

Our goal is to educate others that everyone can garden in some form or another.

Speaking Engagements

We both love to talk about our experiences in the building of the farm. It really has become more than just the physical process of using primarily salvaged and recycled materials to build the barn, chicken coop and other structures. It is about the whole process of becoming a responsible steward of the land and environment.

Whether we are speaking at a Self-Sustainability conference or to a local gardening club, we are often told that our passion for what we do shines through in our down-to-earth approach in speaking to others. It's not hard to figure out, we really do love what we do.

When Jim travels for his 'real job', he meets so many people across the U.S. that share the same desire to live a simpler life and would love to somehow be responsible for growing some of their own food. Their small talk conversations quickly turn to how two professionals took on this challenge and are accomplishing just that and how they could too.

We are honored when people approach us and ask us to speak about and the process of building our self-sustaining farm from scratch using primarily salvaged and recycled materials. We love to share how we completed various DIY projects that have become one of the highlights of our website and some of which have been published in national magazines.

We also have been asked to speak about our various gardening techniques, including raised row gardening, gardening in small spaces, composting and most recently the fledgling concept of the Any Age Anywhere Garden.

That leads us to the conference topics of cooking, canning and preserving, a necessary next step in ensuring that your harvest can last year around. Whether it be preparing meals at home without preservatives or how to use a pressure canner to preserve those green beans, we discuss our approaches on how to make our garden provide for us even in the cold winter months.

We have also presented on how we built a simple blog that was meant for our families to follow along in our journey, to one that now has grown to nearing 20 million hits and tens of thousands subscribers. The ins and outs of the development of this website are discussed and how two people who aren't computer experts in any way, shape, or form, found a way to make it a successful part of their life. We hope to inspire others who want to write about their own journey.

But most importantly, all these topics go back to our main outlook in life that living simple and responsible leads to a more satisfying life. From how to simplify the gardening process to organizing and learning to live with less 'stuff', we demonstrate to others that living with less is much more fulfilling than living with more.

What most people find comforting is that we are typical people working 'real' jobs with 4 children living in Midwest America. We both get up to go to work in the morning and work a full week, yet, we find the time to work towards our dream. This is truly our passion and in the future we hope that this leads the way for inspiring others to live out their dreams as well by living a healthier and happier lifestyle by continuing to publish information on our website, in books, and through speaking engagements.

Thanksgiving 2020 – Bringing it All Home

Hands down – Thanksgiving will always be one of our favorite holidays of the year. This is the one time of the year to have family and friends seated together, enjoying each other's company, catching up and telling stories while sharing a wonderful meal together, with the only gifts required, being ones of companionship and love. Truly what it should all be about!

So each year we rotate which family member will be the host home for the gathering. With the plans in place to build our simple home at the farm in the near future we begin to dream about our turn for hosting one large gathering of family and friends for a future Thanksgiving Dinner at The Farm. Although we grow quite a bit of our own food at the farm, it will still be a few years before some of the long-term plantings like the apple and cherry trees, or the wine and jelly grapes begin bearing sizable yields. So, with that in mind, we picked 2020 as the dream year. And hopefully that dream can become a reality. After all, it wasn't that long, in fact just a few short years ago that Jim and I stood at the top of an overgrown hill and dreamed about the chickens, building a barn and having a garden. With a little work (and sore muscles and a loss of blood now and then) that dream came true. So why not dream a little more!

It truly is a completely different feeling to sit down to a meal that comes from what you have grown or raised. Everything tastes fresher and more pure. Plus, we have the satisfaction of knowing exactly where our food came from and also the work that went into growing it. From the early spring days when we first planted it, to nurturing it throughout the summer months, and then to the proud moment of harvesting, it all comes down to a chance to share them with family and friends. And after all isn't that where those very first traditions of Thanksgiving from the Pilgrim's came from?

So, by that future 2020 date, with a little luck and good fortune, we will be able to serve the first vintages of our home-made wine – made from the Marquette grape vines from our small vineyard. And the apple and cherry trees, along with the pumpkins from that year's garden, will create the pies for dessert. That, of course, will go along with most of the meal prepared with a bounty from the garden including green beans, corn, potatoes, carrots, onions, fresh herbs and more.

So as our little dream continues on for that someday dinner, our thoughts turn to the barn decorated with long farm tables with centerpieces made from our home-grown Indian corn, gourds and pumpkins, it becomes most apparent what we are truly thankful for. This includes the opportunity to have a hand in what we grow and eat and of even more importance, to share it with family and friends.

I am sure that over the next several years we will have many highs and lows in the continued building of the farm. But we also know that nothing can ever stop the power of dreams. So, as we look forward to that Thanksgiving dinner in the year 2020, we will continue to grow, dream, and strive to live the simple life.

Jim and Mary

Appendix

Without the support of these Kickstarter Dream-makers, the writing and publication of this book would not have been possible. We extend a HUGE thank you to each and every one of you for making our dream a reality.

Mike and Brad McMahon
McMahon Truck Centers of Columbus
Rob and Jenn Foehl
KarriAnn Spring
Carolyn Martini Cox
Anne Hadley
William Donovan
Teri Lowe
Christian and Michele Robertson
Georgeann Leber
Shawn Taylor
Deborah Burger
EDR Properties
Michael and Diana Casas Hensley
Matt and Nicole Nicol
Julia Gass
Charles and Toni Cunningham
Dustin Matchett
Breta Stroud
Carlton and Mary Anne Rider
Stephanie Hunsicker
Brad and Holly Wesberry
Howard and Shirley Scarver
Mary Ann Jeppson
Anita Owens
Brad Godsey
Jim and Pattie Weisent
Kelli and Manny Diaz

Carol Harr
Mike, Jill and Jake Evans
Sarah Foehl
Chris and Tonia May
Codi and John
Jeff@HomesteadDad.com
Penny Parkinson
Ed and Donna Parris
Michael Carey
Elaine Hawkins
Brandye
Steve and Therese Karnes
Victoria and Robert Carney
Peter Brennan
Andy and Laura Berger
Susanne Devine
Mary Pillard
Sharon Harmon
Bob Reesen
Rachel
Lisa Cone/Alice Loyd
The Houston Family
Ted V.
Donna and Tom Larussa
Angie Morrison
Marti Fuller
Bonnie and Bill Morton
Miriam Illions
Pam and John Odino
Ann McCarthy
Mary
Dominic Competti
Rita Competti
Dick and Candy Foehl
Jim Butler
Bill Weaver
Dave and Debbie Bell
Chris LaRosa
Becky

Dennis and Zoee Saltzman
Holly McKee
Terri Giometti
Ruth Harper
Tony Gugliemotto
Raelyn Harman Subramanian
Richard Zink
Linda Smith
Jim and Lia Lapekas
James Franklin
Sean Lintow Sr.
Carol Wallace
Jessica Royster
Megan Johnson
Alissa Horstman
Dawna
Karen Saville
Mary Boutwell
Veronica Selz
Vicky Schmitt-Vitali
Teresa Klepac
Charlene Kimbrell
Jim Freeman
Bruno Kieffer
Jeff and Kristen Rider
Amy Oldehoeft
Cheryl Hansberry
Evan and Karen Keller
Carla Hanson
Rich and DeeDee Ball
Reta Price
Vikki James
Tricia Pogue
Cheri Schulzke
Marlene Jensen
Heather Allen
Brenda Hanes
Judith Montgomery
Daphne Cybele

Sara Briechle
Sydelle Denman
Ken and Laura Mulligan
Shirley Hamilton
Danielle Pappas
Randy Patrick
Regina Simons
Josephine Beal
Chewy Fewy
Nancy
Gail Petrillo
Jo Miller
Angie Smith
Marissa Swett
Bill and Susan Lee
NewCastle Custom Homes
Nancy See Swecker
Vivian S. Valtri Burgess
Louann Herman
Mary Beth Jurden
Deb Ray
Ruby Olivia
Carol L Oswald
Christinia Nellemann
Richard Devlin
Rick and Ruth Ann Runyon
Julie Barclay
Tina Williams
Andrew Clark
Kelsey F.
Laura Keegan
Lori Sagar Cheney
Isabella Harmon
Sam Wray
Christy Dougherty
Owen and Aidan Love
André F
Brian Jurden
Donna Waddell

Bonnie
Todd Trahan
Jan B
Tikva Jacob
Mary Hill
Lara Mittaud
Joseph C.